SLAVISTIC PRINTINGS AND REPRINTINGS

edited by

C. H. VAN SCHOONEVELD

Indiana University

275

LANGUAGE AND PROSODY
OF THE
RUSSIAN FOLK EPIC

by

ROY G. JONES

Rice University

1972

MOUTON

THE HAGUE · PARIS

LIBRARY OF CONGRESS CATALOG CARD NUMBER: 72-88176

Printed in The Netherlands by Mouton & Co., Printers, The Hague

TABLE OF CONTENTS

I

METER AND RHYTHM

1. INTERPRETATIONS OF STRESS AS THE BASIS OF METER

Descriptions of *bylina* meter based on the opposition of stressed and unstressed syllables have been of three principal types,[1] those in which only certain stresses are considered to be relevant for defining the meter, those in which all stresses are accepted as having a meter-defining role, and those in which distinctions among stresses are made but no stresses are specifically excluded in defining the meter.

1.1. *Accentual Systems*

A theory of prosody accentual in principle but based on only part of the stresses which occur in a line was first formulated for folk verse by Vostokov. He observed that in speech the degree of stress on a word depends on its function and position in a phrase.[2] He recognized three degrees of stress, or in his words, three kinds of stressed syllables: unstressed, weakly stressed, and syllables with a main stress.[3] Vostokov called the word groups united by the main stresses "prosodic periods". According to his interpretation a line in folk verse is composed of prosodic periods and not of feet. The most characteristic lines of epic verse were held to have three stresses (three prosodic periods) and a dactylic

---

[1] In this study it is assumed that word stress is the organizing principle of the line. Although the *bylina* were accompanied by a melody, the relationship between the melody and syllabic structure of the line is not treated.

For a detailed presentation of the various theories of the prosody of folk verse see M. P. Štokmar, *Issledovanija v oblasti russkogo narodnogo stixosloženija* (Moscow, 1952), pp. 17-135, and Kiril Taranovski's review, *Južnoslovenski filolog*, 21 (1955-1956), pp. 335-363. Also A. M. Astaxova, *Byliny* (Moscow-Leningrad, 1966), pp. 143-162.

[2] A. Vostokov, *Opyt o russkom stixosloženii* (St. Petersburg, 1817), p. 95. Cited from Štokmar, *op. cit.*, p. 36.

[3] *Ibid.*, p. 101. Cited from Štokmar, *op. cit.*, pp. 37-38.

ending.[4] This system is essentially an accentual one, for the meter is described only by the number of stresses in a line while the position of stressed syllables and the number of syllables in a line are disregarded.

Later studies which incorporated Vostokov's assumptions about the prosody of folk verse are mainly attempts to define the nature of the stress uniting the word groups, which were assumed to be the units comprising the line. It seemed necessary to define this stress in such a way that the exclusion of all except the main stresses from consideration in defining the meter would be justified. Therefore, the semantically more important words were said to bear the main stresses. But the possibility of various interpretations of a line and the resulting disagreements as to which words were semantically more important, and consequently which stresses were the main ones, weakened the very basis of the theory.

Goloxvastov called the basic metrical units feet, but they are equivalent to Vostokov's periods. The number of "feet" in a line is not determined by the total number of purely phonological stresses but by the "semantic" (smyslovoe) stresses. His description is not entirely accentual, for he correctly identified the stresses on the third, seventh, and eleventh syllables in the 13-syllable line as the main ones.[5] However, he did not determine the position of stresses in lines of other lengths. Maslov defined the smallest rhythmical unit as the "rhythmic period", with one stress in each.[6] A line contains one main "logical" stress and several secondary ones. There are two epic meters, full and abbreviated.[7] Lines in the full epic meter contain three rhythmic periods with a dactylic ending. The abbreviated form of the epic meter is similar but has a shorter second period. Like Vostokov's, these meters are accentual. Žirmunskij in a recent study states that accentual verse "predominates in Russian folk verse (particularly in the 'byliny')"[8] despite the investigations which have demonstrated the regular occurrence of stress on given syllables in most lines.

---

[4] Ibid., p. 139. Cited from Štokmar, op. cit., p. 40.

[5] P. D. Goloxvastov, Zakony stixa russkogo narodnogo i našego literaturnogo (St. Petersburg, 1883), pp. 45-46.

[6] A. L. Maslov, "Byliny, ix proisxoždenie, ritmičeskij i melodičeskij sklad", Trudy muzykal'no-ètnografičeskoj komissii pri Ètnografičeskom otdele Obščestva ljubitelej estestvoznanija, antropologii i ètnografii, II (Moscow, 1911), p. 311.

[7] Ibid., pp. 315-316.

[8] V. M. Žirmunskij, "The Versification of Majakowski", Poetics, Poetyka, Poètika, II (Warsaw, 1966), p. 212.

1.2. *Descriptions in Terms of Metrical Feet*

When the meter is defined in terms of all stresses or possible stresses in a line, the metrical foot is used to indicate the regular sequence of stressed and unstressed syllables. As defined by Gil'ferding the epics consist predominantly of 5- and 6-foot trochaic lines with a dactylic ending.[9] Since the stresses in these lines appear on odd syllables and all odd syllables may be stressed, this description seems to be appropriate for lines containing an odd number of syllables. But lines with an even number of syllables in *bylina* must be described as consisting of mixed feet. A meter can be defined by mixed feet only if there is a regular repetition of the different feet, which is not found in *bylina*. He attaches no significance to the fact that some syllables are always stressed and others not.

Štokmar regards the meter of the *bylina* as predominantly quaternary.[10] He states that 4-syllable groups predominate but occur along with 3- and 5-syllable and even 2- and 6-syllable groups. He sees a conflict between the quaternary nature of the rhythm of the line and the "dynamic harmony" of the language of the *bylina*, which tends toward 5-syllable groups with a stress on the middle syllable, $--/--$. But combinations of such groups would give sequences of four unstressed syllables between stresses, which is one of the rarest occurring sequences in *bylina*. As he states, the norms of the "dynamic harmony" were determined in the language of the *bylina*, so these norms are not those of non-poetic language as opposed to the language of the *bylina*. The apparent conflict is not between language system and verse system, but arises from the expectation that combinations of the syllable group expressing the "dynamic harmony" should produce the observed interval of unstressed syllables between stressed ones. He states that "if the stress-syllable groups of *bylina* language were formed under the direct influence of *bylina* rhythm, then they would be 4-syllabic and not 5-syllabic."[11] Since there should be a direct relationship between the "dynamic harmony" of the language and the meter, the quaternary meter must be a secondary development.[12] If the unit comprising the line contained five syllables, according to Štokmar there should be a break after each fifth syllable. But no theory of Russian prosody requires that the boundaries

[9] A. F. Gil'ferding, *Onežskie byliny*, 4th ed. (Moscow-Leningrad, 1949), I, p. 66.
[10] Štokmar, *op. cit.*, p. 393.
[11] *Loc. cit.*
[12] *Ibid.*, p. 394.

of the unit expressing the succession of stressed and unstressed syllables coincide with word divisions, as they would have to do to resolve Štokmar's "conflicts".[13] The meter of the 13-syllable lines with three stresses does acquire a quaternary nature, as Taranovski points out.[14] But Štokmar does not discuss lines of other lengths nor designate which syllables are stressed. His description approaches one in terms of mixed feet when he states that 2-, 3-, 5-, and 6-syllable groups occur with the predominant 4-syllable group.

1.3. Descriptions Based on the Foot with Obligatory and Optional Stresses Distinguished

Between these two positions are the studies in which "main" (obligatory) stresses are assigned primary importance in defining the meter, which is still said to be in some way trochaic. Jakobson distinguishes between syllables which are optionally stressed and those which are compulsorily stressed and calls the meter trochaic.[15] He states that the long verses, 13-syllable lines, of North Russian laments, which are metrically similar to the *bylina*, are "centered" on the three main stresses, on the third, seventh and eleventh syllables, e.g., *Ukratílosja velíkoe želánice, Ono v vóduški, zeláne vo glubókii*.[16] He makes the same distinction between obligatory and optional stresses in epic verse but refers to trochaic lines and the trochaic beat of the lines.[17] He notes that the singer Ul'jana was inclined to stress *all* the odd syllables in her laments, which "noticeably modifies the whole meter."[18] Žirmunskij defines meter as the ideal law which governs the alternation of strong and weak syllables (sounds) in verse. The actual alternation in a line is the rhythm.[19] Jakobson does not consider the meter of the laments and *bylina* to be trochaic in the usual sense, for in a trochaic line all the odd syllables may be stressed. The result is coincidence of meter and rhythm, not modification of the meter.

[13] Unbegaun's statement concerning feet is applicable to Štokmar's 5-syllable groups: "...the metrical breaking-up of a line into feet is independent of the real breaking-up of a sentence into words: they need not coincide one with another." B. D. Unbegaun, *Russian Versification* (Oxford, 1956), p. 13.

[14] Taranovski, *op. cit.*, p. 358.

[15] Roman Jakobson, "Studies in Comparative Slavic Metrics", *Oxford Slavonic Papers*, III (1952), p. 39.

[16] *Ibid.*, pp. 36-37.

[17] *Ibid.*, pp. 40-41.

[18] *Ibid.*, pp. 37-38.

[19] V. M. Žirmunskij, *Introduction to Metrics*, trans. C. F. Brown (The Hague, 1966), p. 17.

In his study of the *bylina* Harkins also defines the meter of the 11- and 13-syllable lines in terms of the three main stresses and designates their position. He agrees with Gil'ferding that these lines may be called trochaic in the sense that the stresses occur on odd syllables.[20] In his discussion of irregular lines (those not containing 11 or 13 syllables) he also points out a tendency toward a trochaic rhythm and states that a trochaic rhythm is apparent in them.[21]

2. THE ROLE OF OPTIONAL STRESSES

In none of these studies in which types of stresses are differentiated is the specific function of any except the main stresses explained. For Vostokov only the main stresses are relevant. In Jakobson's analysis the optional stresses at least share with the main stresses in defining the meter. Harkins' scansion of the 11- and 13-syllable lines is affected only by main stresses, but it is not clear if he intends to exclude the other stresses when he writes that a trochaic rhythm is apparent in some lines. The exact role of the optional or weak stresses in the rhythmic structure of the *bylina* is not defined.

2.1. *Optional Stresses Opposed to Obligatory Stresses and Unstressed Syllables*

Even though the optional stresses are usually those of weakly stressed words, such syllables are stressed as opposed to unstressed syllables. However, the fact that the kind of word which bears the optional stresses is restricted to short subsidiary ones indicates that these stresses are opposed in some way to the main stresses. Syllables with these stresses seem to be intermediate between stressed and unstressed. The stress of these syllables differs from the main ones in degree but is like the main stresses in that they occur on odd syllables. In the *bylina* it seems necessary to divide syllables into three types: stressed, weakly stressed, and unstressed. But prosody in a language like Russian consists in the regular alternation of stressed and unstressed syllables. Metrically, syllables are either stressed or unstressed. In meter there is not an intermediate step between the two extremes. Syllables with weak (optional)

---

[20] William Harkins, "O metričeskoj roli slovesnyx formul v serboxorvatskom i russkom èpose", *American Contributions to the Fifth International Congress of Slavists* (The Hague, 1963), II, p. 155.
[21] *Ibid.*, pp. 55-56.

stress must be treated as unstressed and not affecting the meter, as stressed and to some degree helping to define the meter, or interpreted another way.

2.2. *Optional Stresses as Part of Rhythm*

In his discussion of the French Alexandrine line Žirmunskij distinguishes between obligatory and optional stresses and describes the meter in terms of obligatory stress only. He states that "The only metrically regulated feature of the French Alexandrine line is thus the obligatory recurrence of the stress at the end of each hemistich,... Only at the end of the line does the expectation of an *obligatory* stress establish rhythmical *inertia*. All other stresses belong to the area of rhythm and recur in various combinations."[22] Similarly, the optional stresses in *bylina* may be assigned to rhythm. The obligatory stresses define the "ideal law" of alternation of stressed and unstressed syllables. The optional stresses modify the ideal alternation and are thus a part of the rhythm. It is these constant stresses which determine the rhythmical inertia of the line, for the optional stresses are too infrequent to create a rhythmical movement with an expectation of stress on these syllables.

3. DIFFERENCE BETWEEN METER AND RHYTHM IN *BYLINA* AND LEARNED VERSE

The pattern defined by the obligatory stresses is the one into which the singer attempts to fit the words of his *bylina*. He cannot always be successful, for to do so would be to limit himself to using words of a few specific rhythmical types. When he is unsuccessful, stresses appear on other odd syllables. The writer of learned poetry is faced with the same problem, but his deviation from the meter results in the omission of stresses. The relationship between meter and rhythm in the two kinds of verse is illustrated below. The meters are different, but one rhythmic variant of the meter of the 13-syllable line is identical with the meter of a trochaic line with 13 syllables. The same relationship is seen between the meter of the trochaic line and one possible rhythmic variant of the *bylina* meter. "–" and "/" designate unstressed and stressed syllables respectively. Both the writer of learned poetry and the singer of *bylina* must deviate

[22] Žirmunskij, *op. cit.*, p. 77.

	Learned Poetry	*Bylina*
Meter	/-/-/-/-/-/	--/---/---/--
Rhythm	--/---/---/--	/-/-/-/-/-/

from the meter because of the length and stress patterns of Russian words, but the deviations are of opposite kinds, i.e., in learned poetry rhythmic variation is created by the deletion of stresses whereas in *bylina* such variation is created by the addition of stresses.

II

DESCRIPTION OF THE METER

1. INTRODUCTION

This study adopts the position just described, which is a modification of Jakobson's and Harkins' approach. The meter is defined in terms of the obligatory stresses only and the optional stresses are seen as modifying the meter thus established. That this differentiation in function of obligatory and optional stresses leads to a more acceptable description of the meter and rhythm of the *bylina* is demonstrated below in the analysis of almost 3,500 lines from *bylina* recorded in 1871 by Gilferding from T. G. Rjabinin.[1]

1.1. *Repetition of Lines*

Exact repetition of lines is a common occurrence in the *bylina*, but only one occurrence of a given line has been counted in the same *bylina*. Two lines containing the same words but not in the same grammatical forms are considered to be different. If two lines which are otherwise identical contain different particles, they are not considered to be the same. Lines composed of the same words, but in another order are also separate lines. Unless a line is identical in every way with another, it is not considered to be a repetition of that line.

1.2. *Variations at the Beginning and End of the Line*

In determining line length and the positions of the stressed syllables, the syllables in a line were counted as if there were always two unstressed syllables before the first obligatory stress, the anacrusis, and two follow-

---

[1] A. F. Gil'ferding, *Onežskie byliny*, 4th ed., 3 vols. (Moscow-Leningrad, 1949-1951). All lines excluding repetitions, from Nos. 73-85, Vol. II, pp. 4-117 were included. Gil'ferding observed that Rjabinin was among the best singers from whom he recorded *bylina*, Vol. I, p. 69.

ing the last obligatory stress, a dactylic close. For example, a line of twelve syllables with stresses on the second, sixth, and tenth syllables is considered to be a 13-syllable line with the omission of one syllable in the anacrusis. The stressed syllables then become the third, seventh, and eleventh. The number of syllables in the anacrusis varies from zero to four and in the close from two to three unstressed syllables. But such variation is infrequent and the arrangement of stressed and un-stressed syllables within the line is unaffected by it. A melodic accent on the final syllable, stressed or unstressed, of a line is characteristic of performance and is not equivalent to the stresses which define meter and rhythm.

1.3. Obligatory and Optional Stresses

51% of the lines studied contain 13 syllables. (See Table 1, which gives the distribution of the metrically correct lines, 90% of the total, after the exclusion of lines which are repetitions.)

TABLE 1

Length and Frequency of Lines

No. of Syllables in Line	No. of Lines	Percentage
7	2	—
8	9	0.3
9	85	2.5
10	40	1.2
11	1051	30.6
12	195	5.7
13	1755	51.0
14	17	0.5
15	165	4.8
16	4	0.1
17	102	3.0
18	1	—
19	5	0.1
20	2	—
21	4	0.1
25	1	—
Total	3438	99.9

60% of the 13-syllable lines have only three stressed syllables, which always occur on the third, seventh, and eleventh syllables. This fact alone indicates the pivotal nature of stress on these syllables for the meter. Moreover, when other syllables are stressed, the third, seventh, and eleventh are also stressed. The stresses are distributed in the following way:

Syllable	1	3	5	7	9	11	13
%	—	100	32	100	10	100	—

The stress which occurs on the fifth and ninth syllables is usually that of weakly stressed words, which often lose their semantic value and function in *bylina* as particles to provide additional syllables as needed in the line. Almost half of them are monosyllabic, and the stress on words longer than two syllables does not occur here.

A'šče mésto-to	v pirý mnè	bỳlo pó činy	80,163[2]
Na dobróm kone	sidít Il'jà,	ne stáritsja	75,418

The restriction on the kind of words which appear in these positions justifies a division of stressed syllables into main (obligatory) and secondary (optional). This division is further supported by the positions of the breaks which separate the word groups into which the line is divided by the stresses. (See Chapter III).

2. CLASSIFICATION OF THE LINES BY "METERS"

Although the number of syllables in the lines ranges from seven to twenty-five, there are only four different stress arrangements. The lines may be grouped so that each line in a group has the stress arrangement distinctive for that group and differs only in length by a multiple of four syllables from other lines of the group. The composition of the four groups is given below:

Group	No. of Syllables in Line					No. of Lines	Percentage
1	7	11	15	19		1223	35.6
2	8	12	16	20		210	6.1
3	9	13	17	21	25	1947	56.6
4	10	14	18			58	1.7

The number designating a group corresponds to the number of unstressed syllables between two stresses which distinguishes that group. Thus Group 1 lines have a 1-syllable sequence between two of the stresses, Group 2 two, etc. The shortest occurring line of each group contains only the distinguishing feature of that Group, e.g.:

[2] In citation of lines the first figure refers to the number of the *bylina*, the second to the line number, as given by Gil'ferding.

Group 1: $--/-/--$ Stal Vol'gá pokrýkivati   73,158
Group 2: $--/--/--$ Aj že Vol'gá Svjatoslávgovič   73,65
Group 3: $--/---/--$ Kak ot ržán'ja lošadínago   75,197
Group 4: $--/----/--$ Na Opráksii korolévičnoj   81,355

The longer lines of each group contain, in addition, the characteristic feature of Group 3 — obligatory stresses separated by three unstressed syllables, as can be seen from comparing these lines in Group 1.

7   $--/-/--$ Stal Vol'gá pokrýkivati   73,158
11 $--/-/---/--$ Priezžál Dobrýnja iz čistá polja   79,6
15 $--/-/---/---/--$ Ja stojál zaútrenu xristóvskuju vo
                         Múromle   74,168

2.1. *Group 3*

Group 3 makes up 56% of the total number of lines. Most of the lines in the group contain 13 syllables, 90% of Group 3 and 51% of the total. As already mentioned, Gil'ferding indicated that with good singers such as Rjabinin 11- and 13-syllable (5- and 6-foot trochaic) lines predominate.[3] Jakobson states that the 13-syllable line is typical of average narrators, who often deviate from the canon, the 11-syllable line.[4] But he also adds that "it is only to be expected that the symmetrical and more manageable 6-foot variant should easily gain the ascendancy over the 5-foot pattern".[5] This has happened in the *bylina* studied, and the 13-syllable line must be recognized as the basic one.[6]

Distinctive for Group 3 is the separation of all obligatory stresses by three unstressed syllables. The arrangement of the stresses in these lines is given below.[7]

Syllables in Line	Stressed Syllables	Stress Distribution	Number
9	3-7	$--/---/--$	85
13	3-7-11	$--/---/---/--$	1755
17	3-7-11-15	$--/---/---/---/--$	102
21	3-7-11-15-19	$--/---/---/---/---/--$	4
25	3-7-11-15-19-23	$--/---/---/---/---/---/--$	1

[3] Gil'ferding, *op. cit.*, Vol. 1, p. 66.
[4] Roman Jakobson, "Studies in Comparative Slavic Metrics", *Oxford Slavonic Papers* (1952) III, p. 42.
[5] *Ibid.*, p. 44.
[6] The high frequency of the 13-syllable line in Rjabinin's *bylina* is also shown in the study of William Harkins "O metričeskoj roli slovesnyx formul v serboxorvatskom i russkom èpose", *American Contributions to the Fifth International Congress of Slavists* (The Hague, 1963) II, p. 155.
[7] Examples of all lines are given in the Appendix.

Korš points out that long lines are combinations of regular lines with half lines,[8] but this is not always the case. Some stereotyped phrases, such as *vo čistó pole, vo belú ruku*, repeatedly occur, and the number of syllables in a line may be increased by adding one of the phrases. That all longer lines are not formed in this way may be seen from the following examples which do not contain one of these phrases.

Ešče čtó že polágaeš' ty trinádcatyj to pódprug da zapásnyi   80,233
Zaxotélos' na ponóse mne-ka mjása lebedínogo   83,102

The distribution of the stresses in these lines is identical with that in all other lines of Group 3. Expansion of a line is not a mechanical process of addition, for the stereotyped phrases are modified if necessary to conform with the meter of the line to which they are added. And the appearance of the same tendencies in distribution of stresses in long lines as found in the shorter, more frequent ones confirms the existence of such tendencies.

2.2. *Group 1*

The special feature of Group 1 is the separation of two main stresses by a single syllable, between the third and fifth syllables in the 11I line, which is the second most frequent. In 11II lines the stress on the fifth syllable is omitted. The omission of the stress on this syllable occurs almost exclusively when two 5-syllable groups are joined by a connecting particle. This fact and the infrequency of this type of line indicate that the 11-syllable line with an unstressed fifth syllable is a variant of the normal type with three main stresses.[9] The position of the 1-syllable interval between main stresses varies in the longer lines, although it rarely occurs before the final main stress. The positions where it occurs in the *bylina* studied are shown below. In some lines of Groups 1, 2, and 4 the location of the sequence distinctive for the group varies. The variations are designated by Roman numerals.

The 11-syllable line more than any other seems to be describable in terms of trochaic feet, excluding 11III. It appears that the stresses are omitted in this line just as they are in a 5-foot trochaic line of learned poetry, i.e., that the relationship between meter and rhythm is the same in both. Taranovski has shown the similarity in the probability of

[8]   F. E. Korš, "O russkom narodnom stixosloženii", *Sbornik Otdelenija russkogo jazyka i slovesnosti*, LXVII, No. 8 (St. Petersburg, 1901), p. 23.
[9]   See Chapter IV for the discussion of 11III lines.

Syllables in Line	Stressed Syllables	Stress Distribution	No. of Lines	Percentage
7	3-5	--/-/--	2	—
11I	3-5-9	--/-/---/--	791	75
11II	3-9	--/-----/--	167	16
11III	3-6-9	--/--/--/--	93	9
15I	3-5-9-13	--/-/---/---/--	56	34
15II	3-7-9-13	--/---/-/---/--	66	40
15III	3-7-13	--/---/-----/--	40	24
15IV	3-9-13	--/-----/---/--	3	2
19I	3-7-11-13-17	--/---/---/-/---/--	2	—
19II	3-7-11-17	--/---/---/-----/--	2	—
19III	3-7-13-17	--/---/-----/---/--	1	—

stresses occurring on the same syllable in both types of verse.[10] But in learned verse the frequency of stress on the seventh syllable is almost twice as high as in *bylina*, and the stress on the third syllable of the *bylina* line is constant, as it is not in learned verse. The apparent similarity of the meter of 5-foot trochaic lines and the 11-syllable *bylina* lines arises from the treatment of all stresses equally. If the main stresses only are taken to define the meter in *bylina*, Taranovski's Type VII, --/-/---/-, is the only one metrically possible in *bylina*, with Type XI, --/-----/-, an alternant form. The meter of the 5-foot trochaic line is represented by the scheme, /-/-/-/-/-. A rhythmical variant of this meter is the same as the meter of the 11-syllable *bylina* line. Therefore, the observed similarity is one between a rhythmic variant of the 5-foot trochaic meter and the meter of the 11-syllable *bylina* line, and not between the two meters.

Almost 6% of the 11-syllable lines are stressed on the seventh syllable and unstressed on the fifth syllable, --/---/-/--. The stress on the seventh syllable is not equivalent to the one on the fifth syllable, for it is usually on a subsidiary word and rarely on a word longer than two syllables. There are no such restrictions on the word which bears the stress in the fifth syllable. In these as in all 11II lines there is always a break after the fifth syllable. Therefore, these lines are treated as rhythmic variants of the meter of the 11II lines, with an optional stress on the seventh syllable.

2.3. *Group 2*

A line with twelve syllables is the most common in Group 2 and is representative of the group which is distinguished by two main stresses separated by two unstressed syllables. In 12I lines this sequence is found

[10] Kiril Taranovski, *Ruski dvodelni ritmovi* (Belgrade, 1953), p. 280.

between the first two stressed syllables, while in 12II lines it occurs between the last two. The meter of the longer lines of this group is sometimes difficult to determine, but in those where the meter is evident there is a tendency for the sequence to occur at the beginning of the line also. All other main stresses are separated by three syllables as seen below.

Syllables in Line	Stressed Syllables	Stress Distribution	No. of Lines	Percentage
8	3-6	--/--/--	9	—
12I	3-6-10	--/--/---/--	104	53
12II	3-7-10	--/---/--/--	91	47
16	3-6-10-14	--/--/---/---/--	4	—
20	3-6-10-14-18	--/--/---/---/---/--	2	—

2.4. Group 4

Group 4 comprises less than 2% of the total lines. It is characterized by a sequence of four unstressed syllables between two main stresses. This sequence may be broken by an additional stress, and such lines then acquire the features of Group 1 and 2 — main stresses separated by one and by two unstressed syllables.

Syllables in Line	Stressed Syllables	Stress Distribution	No. of Lines	Percentage
10I	3-8	--/----/--	24	60
10II	3-5-8	--/-/--/--	16	40
14I	3-8-12	--/----/---/--	8	47
14II	3-7-12	--/---/----/--	3	18
14III	3-6-8-12	--/--/-/---/--	6	35
18I	3-5-8-12-16	--/-/--/---/---/--	1	—

The longer lines of this group rarely occur, and it is difficult to determine which types are to be considered the norm.

3. BASIC METRICAL TENDENCIES

3.1. Distribution of Stresses

Three syllables between stresses is the feature characterizing Group 3, which makes up a majority of the lines, and this is the only feature which occurs in all groups. It is the only feature which may be repeated in a line, for the features which characterize the other groups may appear in a line only once. Therefore, the primary metrical tendency in *bylina* is for stressed syllables to be separated by three unstressed ones. The frequency of Group 1 indicates that intervals of odd numbers of unstressed syllables are metrically more acceptable than longer sequences of an even number of syllables, as in Group 2. A sequence of four unstressed syllables, alternating with two stresses separated by one syllable and two separated by two syllables as in Group 4, is barely tolerated and appears in less than 2% of the lines.

3.2. *Infeasibility of Descriptions in Terms of Feet*

It is impossible to describe the meter of this variety of lines by a single kind of foot. Descriptions in terms of either trochaic or quaternary feet are the most likely possibilities, but neither is acceptable. A description in terms of trochaic feet obscures the difference in nature and function between optional and obligatory stresses and does not in fact describe meter but merely indicates that most stresses occur on odd syllables. Lines with an even number of syllables, Groups 2 and 4, cannot be described by trochaic feet since even syllables are stressed in them. A quaternary foot indicates the most frequent distribution of stresses in all lines, and the distribution of all the stresses in lines of Group 3, three unstressed syllables between two stressed ones. But if a quaternary foot is to be used in the description of *bylina* meter, it must be re-defined so that it may contain a secondary stress in addition to the main one, which the traditional definition of the foot does not allow. If this qualification to the usual definition is permitted, Group 3 lines can be described as combinations of the second paeon with an additional syllable preceding the first foot or the third paeon with an extra syllable following the last foot. Lines of other groups would have to be described as having one paeon replaced by another foot, i.e., in terms of mixed feet. The stress distribution may be better described by designating the stressed syllables in each line type as a whole. Since the stresses in the most frequent lines always fall on the same syllables, the meter is implied by the line length. Thus, the number "13" designates a 13-syllable line with stresses on the third, seventh and eleventh syllables, "11I" an 11-syllable line with stressed third, fifth, and ninth syllables, "12I" a 12-syllable line with stressed third, sixth, and tenth syllables, etc.

The variability in line length, combined with the fixed beginning and ending of the line, contributes to the difficulty in describing the meter in terms of feet. Lines containing eleven and thirteen syllables make up almost 75% of the total, but it seems unjustified to regard lines of other lengths as metrically irregular solely because of length, especially those in Groups 1 and 3 which have the same features of stress distribution as the 11- and 13-syllable lines. Since all lines differ only in the number of syllables between two stressed syllables, and since there is a fixed arrangement of stresses at the beginning and end of the line, the change in number of syllables between these two stresses is dependent on the change in number of syllables in the line. Therefore, no lines are regarded as irregular in this study unless there is random distribution of stresses. Moreover, variation in line length may be considered as a means of introducing variety into the *bylina*. Optional stresses may occur, but this modification of meter is not of the same order as the omission of metrical stresses in learned poetry, and the number of possible variants of a *bylina* line is much smaller than a line in learned verse. Isosyllabic verse with little possibility of rhythmic variation would be monotonous. To overcome this difficulty and achieve rhythmic variety, the singer may vary the length of the lines. Thus, variation in line length may not be a caprice of the singer or an indication of lack of poetic skill but rather a solution to the problem of rhythmical monotony which could result if all lines were isosyllabic.

III

RHYTHMIC UNITS COMPOSING THE LINES

1. INTRODUCTION

The number of words composing a line is the same as the number of main stresses in a line which does not contain optional stresses, since words in Russian contain only one stress. The accentual pattern of these words is the form of the rhythmic units which comprise the line. When optional stresses occur, they are subordinated to one of the main stresses, and the number of units is not changed by them. In some lines the position of breaks depends on whether particles and words with optional stress are considered to be enclitic or proclitic. For the sake of consistency in such cases, rules based partly on the structure of lines without particles were followed. A word with optional stress on a syllable immediately adjacent to a syllable bearing a main stress is subordinated to that main stress. When monosyllables immediately precede or follow a syllable with main stress, they are proclitic and enclitic, respectively. Other monosyllables are enclitic if they are preceded and followed by one unstressed syllable. They are proclitic if they are preceded by two unstressed syllables and followed by one or preceded and followed by two. Disyllabic words and particles are proclitic if they immediately precede a main stress; they are enclitic if they immediately follow one. Prepositions are always proclitic. The units which result from the application of these rules are the same as those in lines without particles or words with optional stresses.

2. TYPES OF LINES BASED ON COMBINATIONS OF COLONS

2.1. *Group 3*

When the 13-syllable line contains only the obligatory stresses, as it does in 60% of its occurrences, it is divided into three segments whose boundaries are coincident with word divisions. The breaks always occur before and after the fifth and ninth syllables and divide the line into three segments or colons, containing three to five syllables, $--/--$, $-/--$, $-/-$, $--/-$. There are four types of 13-syllable lines, depending on the combination of colons:

13a $--/--$ $-/-$ $--/--$	Da j vo slávnyja poláty belokámenny	79,33
13b $--/-$ $--/-$ $--/--$	Ego sérdce bogatýrsko ne užáxnulos'	79,128
13c $--/--$ $-/--$ $-/--$	Stal molóden'koj Dobrýnjuško Mikítinec	79,3
13d $--/-$ $--/--$ $-/--$	Da j mužík-ot derevénščina ne slúšatsja	74,133

When optional stresses occur, and therefore additional breaks, there are still breaks before or after these syllables.

13a I sadílsja tùt	Il'já da	na dobrá konja		75,185
13b Èto délo	u nàs búdet	nexoróšee		75,297
13c Berét-to òn	ix túgoj lùk	rozrývčatyj		80,490
13d Da spustíl òn	ètu stréločku	kalénuju		75,542

Thus the occurrence of breaks before or after the fifth and ninth syllables is compulsory, just as the stresses on the third, seventh, and eleventh syllables are compulsory even when optional stresses appear on other syllables. The other lines of Group 3 are composed of combinations of only these four colon types. Lines of nine syllables contain two colons, 13-syllable lines three, 17-syllable lines four, etc. In Group 3 the breaks appear before or after the middle syllable between two main stresses as shown in Table 2.

Goloxvastov correctly determined the position of the stresses in the 13-syllable line,[1] but his analysis of the number of syllables in the three parts of the line, "feet" in his terminology, is unacceptable. He stated that the minimum number of syllables in the first colon is three. If it contained fewer than three syllables, it would not include the third syllable, which has the first main stress. The maximum is six syllables, for a number greater than six would include the seventh syllable, which is the position of the second main stress. The possible structure of the last colon is similar to the first, while the second may contain from one to seven syllables. Theoretically, colons of these types are possible, but they do not in fact occur.

---

[1] P. D. Goloxvastov, *Zakony stixa russkogo narodnogo i našego literaturnogo* (St. Petersburg, 1883), p. 45.

TABLE 2
Group 3

Line Type	Line Structure	Stressed Syllables	Position of Breaks*	No. of Lines	Frequency† %
9Ia		3-7	4	41	51
9Ib		3-7	5	40	49
9II		3-5-7	3-5	4	—
13a		3-7-11	5-8	653	37
13b		3-7-11	4-8	266	15
13c		3-7-11	5-9	620	35
13d		3-7-11	4-9	216	12
17a		3-7-11-15	5-9-12	29	28
17b		3-7-11-15	4-9-12	10	10
17c		3-7-11-15	5-8-12	6	6
17d		3-7-11-15	4-8-12	2	2
17e		3-7-11-15	5-9-13	31	30
17f		3-7-11-15	4-9-13	11	11
17g		3-7-11-15	5-8-13	7	7
17h		3-7-11-15	4-8-13	6	6
21a		3-7-11-15-19	4-9-13-16	1	—
21b		3-7-11-15-19	5-9-13-16	1	—
21c		3-7-11-15-19	4-9-13-17	1	—
21d		3-7-11-15-19	5-9-12-17	1	—
25		3-7-11-15-19-23	5-9-12-17-20	1	—

* The syllable after which the breaks occur.

† Frequency is calculated on the basis of the number of lines having a given distribution of the stresses, e.g., the frequency of 9Ia lines is calculated from the total number of 9I lines.

2.2. *Group 1*

Most lines in Group 1 have two main stresses separated by only one syllable and all the others by three. However, 16% of the 11-syllable lines (11II) contain only two stresses, on the third and ninth syllables, and consequently two colons. (See Table 3). Evidence has already been presented which shows that the normal 11-syllable line has three main stresses. In the 11II line with only two stresses the first colon always contains five syllables, the last six. The unique appearance of a 6-syllable colon in these and similar Group 1 lines gives further support to the suggestion that 11-syllable lines with two stresses are modifications of the basic type, 11I, with three stresses. If a line of two colons were taken as the norm for the 11-syllable line, the word with the stress in the fifth syllable would be a part of the colon formed by the stress in the third syllable. Since there is no restriction on the kind of word whose stress may occur in the fifth syllable, this stress is not an optional one. If the stress in the fifth syllable occurred on a 4-syllable word, a 7-syllable colon would be formed. A colon of this length would incorporate an accentual group identical with accentual groups found elsewhere which are unquestionably independent colons. Therefore, such sequences are better interpreted as two colons, one of which is a shortened form of a longer colon, conditioned by this proximity of two main stresses. The modified colons have the forms "/–", "/– –", "–/", "– –/". The colons with an unstressed initial syllable occur only in 12II and 15II lines.

2.3. *Groups 2 and 4*

The main stresses in the lines of Groups 2 and 4 unite accentual groups of the same type as occur in Groups 1 and 3. The unmodified forms of the colons occur when stresses are separated by three syllables, while the shortened forms appear when sequences of fewer than three syllables separate the stresses. (See Tables 4 and 5).

3. POSITIONS OF BREAKS WITH REGARD TO OBLIGATORY STRESSES

In all lines where stresses are separated by three unstressed syllables, breaks always occur before or after the middle syllable between them. Even when the middle syllable bears an optional stress, and therefore additional breaks occur, breaks still appear in these positions. Thus it is clear that breaks here are a part of the structure of the rhythm and are located with respect to the stresses which always occur. The con-

TABLE 3 — Group 1

Line Type	Line Structure	Stressed Syllables	Position of Breaks*	No. of Lines	Frequency †%
7		3-5	4	4	—
11Ia		3-5-9	3-6	276	35
11Ib		3-5-9	4-6	181	23
11Ic		3-5-9	3-7	215	27
11Id		3-5-9	4-7	119	15
11II		3-9	5	167	—
11IIIa		3-6-9	4-6	18	19
11IIIb		3-6-9	3-6	5	6
11IIIc		3-6-9	4-7	40	43
11IIId		3-6-9	5-7	18	19
11IIIe		3-6-9	3-7	4	4
11IIIf		3-6-9	4-8	8	9
15Ia		3-5-9-13	4-7-10	18	32
15Ib		3-5-9-13	3-7-10	11	20
15Ic		3-5-9-13	4-6-10	1	2
15Id		3-5-9-13	3-6-10	4	7
15Ie		3-5-9-13	4-7-11	7	13
15If		3-5-9-13	3-7-11	10	18
15Ig		3-5-9-13	3-6-11	5	9
15IIa		3-7-9-13	5-8-10	12	18
15IIb		3-7-9-13	4-8-10	5	8
15IIc		3-7-9-13	5-7-10	11	17
15IId		3-7-9-13	4-7-10	5	8
15IIe		3-7-9-13	5-8-11	10	15
15IIf		3-7-9-13	4-8-11	2	3
15IIg		3-7-9-13	5-7-11	12	18
15IIh		3-7-9-13	4-7-11	9	14
15IIIa		3-7-13	5-9	32	80
15IIIb		3-7-13	4-9	8	20
15IV		3-9-13	5-10	3	—
19Ia		3-7-11-13-17	4-9-11-14	1	—
19Ib		3-7-11-13-17	5-9-12-15	1	—
19IIa		3-7-11-17	5-9-13	1	—
19IIb		3-7-11-17	4-8-13	1	—
19III		3-7-13-17	5-9-14	1	—

* The syllable after which the breaks occur. † Frequency is calculated on the basis of the number of lines having a given distribution of the stresses, e.g., the frequency of 11Ia is calculated from the total number of 111 lines.

TABLE 4
Group 2

Line Type	Line Structure	Stressed Syllables	Position of Breaks*	No. of Lines	Frequency† %
8a	–/ –/––	3-6	3	1	11
8b	–/ –/––	3-6	4	6	67
8c	–/– –/–	3-6	5	2	22
12Ia	–/– –/ –/––	3-6-10	4-7	27	26
12Ib	–/– –/– –/––	3-6-10	5-7	11	11
12Ic	–/ –/– –/––	3-6-10	3-7	10	10
12Id	–/– –/ –/––	3-6-10	4-8	27	26
12Ie	–/– –/– –/––	3-6-10	5-8	20	19
12If	–/ –/– –/––	3-6-10	3-8	9	9
12IIa	–/– –/ –/––	3-7-10	5-7	40	44
12IIb	–/– –/ –/––	3-7-10	4-7	8	9
12IIc	–/– –/– –/––	3-7-10	5-8	34	37
12IId	–/ –/– –/––	3-7-10	4-8	9	10
16Ia	–/– –/ –/ –/––	3-6-10-14	4-8-11	3	—
16Ib	–/– –/– –/ –/––	3-6-10-14	5-8-12	1	—
20Ia	–/ –/– –/ –/– –/––	3-6-10-14-18	3-7-12-15	1	—
20Ib	–/– –/ –/– –/ –/––	3-6-10-14-18	4-8-12-16	1	—

* The syllable after which the breaks occur.
† Frequency is calculated on the basis of the number of lines having a given distribution, e.g., the frequency of 8a is calculated from the total number of 8-syllable lines.

TABLE 5
Group 4

Line Type	Line Structure	Stressed Syllables	Position of Breaks*	No. of Lines	Frequency† %
10I	--/-- --/--	3-8	5	24	—
10IIa	--/ -/ --/--	3-5-8	3-6	11	69
10IIb	--/ -/ --/--	3-5-8	4-6	2	12
10IIc	--/ --/-- --/--	3-5-8	3-7	3	19
14Ia	--/-- --/-- --/--	3-8-12	5-9	4	
14Ib	--/-- --/-- --/--	3-8-12	5-10	4	
14II	--/-- --/-- --/--	3-7-12	5-9	3	
14IIIa	--/ -/ --/-- --/--	3-6-8-12	4-6-9	4	
14IIIb	--/ -/ --/-- --/--	3-6-8-12	4-6-10	2	
18	--/ --/-- --/-- --/--	3-5-8-12-16	3-6-10-14	1	

* The syllable after which the breaks occur.
† Frequency is calculated on the basis of the number of lines having a given distribution, e.g., the frequency of 10IIa is calculated from the total number of 10II lines.

stant appearance of breaks in these positions, independently of the presence or absence of other breaks formed by the occurrence of optional stresses, indicates that these breaks mark the boundaries between main accentual groups and shows that the stresses uniting these groups are the main ones.

4. FACTORS AFFECTING LOCATION OF BREAKS

The frequency of breaks in a given position is influenced by the number of syllables between stresses and also by the position of the stresses with regard to the beginning or the end of the line.

4.1. *Three-Syllable Intervals*

In the 9-syllable line with two stresses, 9I, the break is slightly more often located before the middle syllable between the two stressed syllables, 51% and 49%. (See Table 6). Except for 12I, 15II, and 17 syllable lines, the same relationship obtains between the last two stresses of the longer lines. However, the break is more frequent after this syllable between the first two stresses of longer lines. Thus, the position of the break in the 9-syllable line is analogous to that in the final part of the longer lines. The beginning or end of the line should not influence the location of the break between the second and third stresses in lines containing four stresses, as in 15I and 17. The break in these lines is much more frequent after the middle syllable than before it, 82% in 15I and 79% in 17-syllable lines.

4.2. *Two-Syllable Intervals*

Two-syllable sequences occur in Groups 1, 2, and 4. The 11III and 12I lines are the only types which are numerous enough for reliable frequencies of the breaks between the first and second stresses to be determined. In both types of lines the break occurs most frequently between the two syllables, in 71% of the 11III lines and 52% of the 12I. In the 11III type the break is located before the two syllables in 10% of the lines and after them in 19%. For the 12I line the frequencies are 19% before and 30% after. Lines of ten syllables which have three stresses contain a 2-syllable sequence between the last two stresses. The break occurs between them in 81% of the lines and after them in 19%. In 11III and 12II lines the last two stresses are also separated by two unstressed syllables. The break more frequently, 67%, occurs between the two syl-

TABLE 6

Location of breaks

Group	Line	Beginning						Medial				End					
		Syll.*	%	Syll.	%	Syll.	%	Syll.	%	Syll.	%	Syll.	%	Syll.	%	Syll.	%
1	11I	3	62	4	38									6	58	7	42
	11III	3	10	4	71	5	19							7	67	8	8
	15I	3	54	4	46			6	18	7	82			10	61	11	39
	15II			4	32	5	68	7	56	8	44			10	50	11	50
2	12I	3	19	4	52	5	30							7	46	8	54
	12II			4	19	5	81							7	53	8	47
3	9I			4	51	5	49					6	25	8	52	9	48
	13			4	28	5	72							12	46	13	54
	17			4	29	5	71							6	81	7	19
4	10II	3	88	4	12			8	21	9	79						

Position in Line

* The syllable after which the break occurs.

lables in the 11III lines but before them in the 12II, 53%. Thus at the beginning of the line a break is more likely to occur between the two syllables in a sequence of two unstressed syllables separating main stresses. However, at the end of the line the most frequent position of the break varies. It may precede the two syllables or occur between them, depending on the type of line. Lines with two syllables between non-final second and third stresses are too infrequent to determine the frequencies.

4.3. *One-Syllable Intervals*

The break between two stresses at the beginning of the line and separated by one syllable as in Groups 1 and 4 are more frequent before this syllable, 62% in the 11I line, 88% in the 10-syllable and 54% in 15I lines. In 15II where the second and third stresses are separated by one syllable, the break is also more frequent before this syllable, 56%.

4.4. *Four-Syllable Intervals*

Sequences of more than three syllables between stresses are rare. There are 24 10-syllable and 11 14-syllable lines in Group 4, which contain a 4-syllable sequence. In all of them the break is in the middle of the sequence between two unstressed syllables.

4.5. *Five-Syllable Intervals*

The occurrence of five consecutive unstressed syllables is restricted, as was pointed out above. The middle syllable in the sequence is usually a particle which has been treated as proclitic. Thus the break occurs before this syllable, and the following stress is preceded by three unstressed syllables. Approximately 16% of the 11-syllable lines are of this type.

4.6. *Basic Tendencies in Locating Breaks*

The frequency of the break before a single unstressed syllable between two stresses, as in 11I, shows the tendency to avoid beginning a colon with a stressed syllable. The 12I lines show that there is a tendency against ending a colon with a stressed syllable, since the frequency of the break between the two unstressed syllables separating two main stresses is similar to that of the break before a single syllable separating two stresses. The break in 3-syllable sequences at the beginning of the line occurs most frequently after the middle syllable of the sequence. The same tendency is observed at the end of the line but with less consistency. Although 4-syllable sequences are very rare, the occurrence of the break so that it is preceded by two unstressed syllables and followed by two points to a tendency for syllabic symmetry in the composition of the colons.

5. FREQUENCY OF COLON TYPES

The mechanism behind the distribution of breaks is more evident if the combinations of colon types which the breaks form are examined, since the formation of the colon types results from the interaction of these tendencies and their frequencies from the relative strength of the tendencies.

5.1. *Terminal Positions*

A majority of the initial colons in all the lines with an appropriate distribution of stresses has five syllables. (See Table 7).

In Group 3 the initial colon contains five syllables in 72% of the 13- and 17-syllable lines. However, the frequency of this colon at the beginning of 9I lines is only 49%. Because of the position of the first two main stresses in 11I and 15I lines, the first colon cannot contain five syllables. 15II lines with three unstressed syllables between the first two stresses occur with a 5-syllable initial colon at a frequency similar to that of 13- and 17-syllable lines, 68%. 12I and 11III with two unstressed syllables between the first two stresses more often begin the line with a 4-syllable colon 52% and 71%, respectively. A 5-syllable initial colon in these lines would necessitate beginning the second colon with a stressed syllable. This type of colon is avoided even when one unstressed syllable separates the first two stresses, as in 11I and 15I. 12II lines have an initial 5-syllable colon in 81% of the lines.

The most frequent colon at the end of the line also contains five syllables. 11I and 15I lines have the highest frequency, 58% and 61%, while only half the 15II lines have a 5-syllable colon in final position. All 11II lines have an initial colon of five syllables and a final one of six. Only 25% of the 11III lines have a 5-syllable colon in final position. In 12I lines a final colon of four syllables is more frequent than a 5-syllable colon, but in 12II lines a 5-syllable colon appears more frequently. Except for those of seventeen syllables, a majority of each line type in Group 3 has a final colon containing five syllables. The few

TABLE 7
Frequency (%) of Colon Types

Position Colon Type	Initial			Medial								Final		
	--/	-/-	-/--	/-	/--	-/	--/	/-	-/-	--/	-/-	--/	-/-	/--
Group 1														
1I	62	38	—	23	15	—	—	35	27	—	—	58	42	—
1III	10	71	19	19	—	19	5	43	9	—	4	25	66	9
1SI	54	46	—	2*	45*	—	—	16* 52†	37* 30†	9†	9†	61	39	—
1SII	—	32	68	26†	18†	35*	21*	33* 24†	32†	—	11*	50	50	—
Group 2														
12I	18	52	30	11	19	—	—	26	26	9	10	46	54	—
12II	—	19	81	—	—	44	9	37	—	—	10	53	47	—
Group 3														
9I	—	51	49	—	—	—	—	37	35	13	15	51	49	—
13	—	28	72	—	—	—	—	13*	59*	20*	8*	52	48	—
17	—	28	72	—	—	—	—	38†	41†	13†	8†	46	54	—
Group 4														
10II	88	12	—	12	—	—	—	69	19	—	—	—	81	19

* Second Colon.
† Third Colon.

10II lines in Group 4 more often end the line with a 4-syllable colon.

A final 5-syllable colon is more frequent in all lines except 10II, 11III, 12I, 15II, and 17. A majority of the total number of lines has a 5-syllable colon at the end of the line, since the number of these line types is small compared to the total. However, the frequency of a 5-syllable colon is less at the end of the line than it is at the beginning. When the distribution of stresses at the beginning of the line permits, a majority of all line types begins the line with a 5-syllable colon. However, at the end of the line a 4-syllable colon is more frequent in some of the lines which have a stress distribution suitable for a 5-syllable colon.

5.2. *Medial Positions*

Within the line a colon of five syllables is very infrequent, for even in the 15- and 17-syllable lines, which are the longest whose occurrences are high enough to determine frequencies, the occurrence of such a colon within the line is limited by the tendency for the initial and final colons to contain five syllables. Lines 13b, $--/- --/- --/--$, (15%), and 13d, $--/- --/-- -/--$ (12%), which do not have an initial colon of five syllables are more infrequent than 13a, $--/-- -/- --/--$ (37%), and 13c, $--/-- -/-- -/--$ (35%), which do. An initial colon of fewer than five syllables seems to be associated with the infrequency of 13b and 13d, since it is the one feature they share and since each shares one feature, the form of the final colon, of 13a or 13c, which are of approximately the same frequency. In the 17-syllable lines the frequency of colon types in initial and final positions is very close to that of 13-syllable lines, while the frequency of the third colon is similar to that of the second colon of the 13-syllable line. Comparison of the frequencies of 17a, $--/-- -/-- -/- --/--$ (28%), with 17c, $--/-- -/- --/- --/--$ (6%), and of 17e, $--/-- -/-- -/-- -/--$ (30%), with 17g, $--/-- -/- --/-- -/--$ (7%), indicates that a shorter initial colon is not the only reason for the infrequency of a line. Both 17a and 17c have initial and final colons of five syllables, but 17a is more frequent than 17c. Lines 17e and 17g have initial colons containing five syllables, but the frequency of 17e is much higher than that of 17g. Each pair differs in the form of the second and third colons. The feature which lessens the frequency of 17c and 17g seems to be the 2-syllable sequence before the third stressed syllable (or the single syllable after the second). Lines 17d with three and 17h with two such medial colons are the most infrequent ones.

5.3. *Basic Tendencies in Colon Types*

The location of the break between the second and third stresses of the 17-syllable line is not influenced by the beginning or end of the line, with the result that the second colon tends to have a dactylic ending. The infrequency of 13b, 13d, 17c, 17d, 17g, and 17h may be explained by the fact that they contain colons not having a dactylic ending. Excluding the second colon from the end, the higher the number of such colons in a line, the lower its frequency. Line 17d has the maximum number and is the most infrequent. Conversely, the lines with the most colons having a dactylic ending are the most frequent, 17a and 17e. Consequently, the basic internal rhythm tends towards colons of the form "–/––", which incorporates the tendencies to precede a stressed syllable with one unstressed syllable and to follow it with two. This tendency helps to explain why an initial colon of five syllables is more frequent than one with four: an initial colon with four syllables cannot have a dactylic ending.

However, a majority of the total number of lines has a prefinal colon which ends with a single unstressed syllable. It appears that the tendency toward colons having a dactylic ending does not apply to the second colon from the end. Or in other words, that there is a slightly stronger tendency toward the appearance of a 5-syllable colon in final position than toward all colons having a dactylic ending. The rhythm of the end of the line seems to conflict with the internal rhythm.

Phrases of ancient formation of the type *vo čistó pole* have been preserved in the *bylina*. They are key expressions in the narrative and are often repeated. They usually contain five syllables and most frequently occur at the end of the line. The colon which precedes one of these phrases cannot end with two unstressed syllables since the stress of the following colon is preceded by two. The frequent appearance of such phrases at the end of the line may explain why the prefinal colon seems not to follow the general tendency for colons to have a dactylic ending.

IV

METRICAL AND RHYTHMICAL CHARACTERISTICS
OF THE INDIVIDUAL *BYLINA*

1. INTRODUCTION

The preceding chapters have presented the general metrical and rhythmical features which characterize the verse of Rjabinin. The extent to which the individual *bylina* exhibit these features may be seen in Figures 1-13 where the average frequency of lines and their rhythmical variants are contrasted with the frequency in each *bylina*. There are two graphs for each *bylina*. The first, A, contrasts the frequency of the most common lines, of 9-13, 15, and 17 syllables; the second, B, compares the frequency of the different rhythmic types of 11-, 12-, and 13-syllable lines, which make up almost 90% of the total number of lines.

2. METRICALLY AND RHYTHMICALLY RELATED *BYLINA*

2.1. *Average Occurrence of Metrical and Rhythmic Features*

The most apparent feature of the average curve in graph A is the high frequency of the 11- and 13-syllable lines, 31% and 51% respectively.[1] The 12-syllable line is third in frequency but comprises only 6% of the total. Graph B shows the similar kind of variation (increase or decrease) in average frequency between structurally analogous lines in 11I and 13-syllable lines. For example, 11Ia is more frequent than 11Ib, and 13a is more frequent than 13b. The structural reason for the higher frequency of a-type lines is the fact that the stress of the second colon is preceded by a single unstressed syllable, while the b-type lines do not have this kind of second colon. A similar relationship exists between 11Ic and 11Id lines and between 13c and 13d lines. The 11II line is more frequent that 11III because it does not contain sequences of an

---

[1] Percentages in graph A are given to the nearest 1%, those in graph B to the nearest 0.5%. See pp. 48-54.

even number of unstressed syllables, as 11III does. Both 12I and 12II contain a sequence of an even number of unstressed syllables. In 12I lines the sequence occurs at the beginning of the lines, while it appears at the end of 12II lines. When a sequence of fewer than three unstressed syllables occurs in a line, it tends to be at or near the beginning of the line as in 11I, 15I, and 15II. Therefore, 12I is more frequent than 12II.

2.2. *Deviation from the Average Curve*

Three *bylina* differ markedly from the rest by their high frequency of 12-syllable lines, and the *bylina* may be divided into two groups on this basis. Those with a low frequency of 12-syllable lines will be called group A, those with a high frequency group B. *Bylina* in group A may be further divided into three subgroups on the basis of similarity in frequency of certain line types. The *bylina* which are most similar are grouped together, but *bylina* in different subgroups may share a feature which is not considered to be significant enough to change the classification. For example, No. 79 in subgroup 1 and No. 76 in subgroup 3 both have higher than average frequencies of 11Ia lines. But a more characteristic feature of No. 79 is the high frequency of 13Ic, and No. 76 has a 13Ic frequency which is lower than the average. Characteristic of No. 76 and the subgroup to which it belongs is the overall high frequency of 11-syllable lines.

2.3. *Group A. Lines with Low Frequency of 12-Syllable Lines*

Subgroup 1. High frequency of 13c lines. Nos. 78, 79, 80, and 85.
    No. 80. "Dobrynja i Vasilij Kazimirov". All the lines of this *bylina* conform more closely than any other to the average frequency. Lines of nine syllables show no deviation from the average. The percentage of 10-syllable lines is also the same. The number of 11-syllable and 12-syllable lines is slightly lower than the average, while the frequency of 13-syllable lines is above.
    The frequency of the rhythmic variants of 11I lines is very close to the average. 11Ia is 1% above the average. There is no difference in 11Ib lines. 11Ic decreases by 0.5%; 11Id increases by the same amount. 11II lines decrease by 1% and 11III by 1.5%. The number of 12-syllable lines is very small, 1% for 12I and 0.5% for 12II. The percentage of 13a lines is 0.5% lower than the average, 13b 2.5% higher. 13c lines increase 2%, while the frequency of 13d is 0.5% low.

No. 78. "Dobrynja i Marinka". The frequencies of the 9- and 12-syllable lines do not deviate from the average. Lines of ten and of fifteen syllables do not occur in this *bylina*. 11-syllable lines are slightly below average and 13-syllable lines considerably above. The frequency of lines containing seventeen syllables is 1.5% above the average.

Two of the variants of 11-syllable lines have frequencies higher than the average and two have lower. 11Ia and 11Ib are below 2.5% and 2% respectively. 11Ic is above by 2.5%, 11Id by 1%. Lines 11II and 11III have the same frequency, 2.5%. 11II is 2.5% below the average, while 11III coincides with the average. 12I lines decrease 0.5%, while 12II increase 1%. The striking features of this *bylina* are the 4% low frequency of 13a lines and the 12% higher frequency of 13c lines. The frequency of 13b is 1% low and that of 13d 1.5% high.

No. 79. "Dobrynja i Zmej". There are no 9- or 10-syllable lines in this *bylina*. The frequencies of 11- and 13-syllable lines are above the average, while those of 12- and 15-syllable lines are below. The percentage of 17-syllable lines is the same.

With the exception of 11Ia, which is 4.5% higher than the average, 11I and 11II lines conform within 1% to the average. There are no 11III lines. The frequency of 12I lines is only 0.5%, 2.5% low; that of 12II only slightly higher, 1%, 1.5% low. All the varieties of 13-syllable lines are above the average frequencies, 13a by 0.5%, 13b by 1.5%, 13c by 5.5%, and 13d by 2%.

No. 85. "Djuk". The number of 9-syllable lines is below average. Lines of ten and twelve syllables do not occur. 11-syllable lines do not deviate from the average. The increase in 13-syllable lines is 5.0%. The frequencies of both 15- and 17-syllable lines are above average.

The distribution of 11-syllable line types is very similar to the average curve. 11Ia and 11Ib are 1% above average, 11Ic 0.5%. 11Id is low by 1% and 11II is high by 1%. There is a 1.5% decrease in 11III lines. Both 13a and 13c lines increase, 13a by 3.5% and 13c by 5%. The frequency of 13b is 3% low, that of 13d 1.5%.

These *bylina* deviate in similar ways from the average curve. The most significant deviation is the increased frequency of 13c lines, which are the most numerous types in these *bylina*. The relationship between 13a and 13c is reversed, for the number of 13a lines usually exceeds the number of 13c.

The hero of Nos. 78, 79, and 80 is *Dobrynja*, whose name very frequently appears in the diminutive form *Dobrynjuška*. When the diminutive occurs in the middle of a line of 13-syllables, a 13c type line is formed, since the rhythmic structure of the diminutive, –/––, is the same as the second colon of 13c lines. Recurrence of a few such key words with the same rhythmic structure could cause the observed deviation from the average pattern in these *bylina*.

Subgroup 2. Low frequency of 11-syllable lines; high frequency of 13-syllable lines. Nos. 74 and 77.

No. 74. "Il'ja Muromec i Solovej Razbojnik". Lines of nine syllables are slightly below average. 10-syllable lines do not occur. There is a decrease of 9% in frequency of 11-syllable lines. An even greater increase of 13-syllable lines is observed, 17%. Only 1% of the lines contain 12 syllables, compared to an average of 6%. The frequencies of 15-syllable and 17-syllable lines are both 4.0%, a frequency which is 1.0% low for 15-syllable lines and 1.0% high for 17-syllable.

All varieties of 11- and 12-syllable lines are from 0.5% to 3% below the average, except 11Id which has the average frequency. No. 11III and 12II lines occur. There is a great increase in the number of 13a lines, 34% instead of 19%. 13b is 0.5% and 13c 2% above the expected frequency. The percentage of 13d is 1.5% low.

No. 77. "Il'ja Muromec i Doč' ego". All the lines except those of thirteen syllables decrease from the average. 9- and 10-syllable lines are both 1% below. Lines of eleven syllables are less frequent than the average by 6%, those of twelve by 5.0%. Lines of fifteen and seventeen syllables are 1% below average. The frequency of 13-syllable lines is 16% above average.

Of the variants of 11-syllable lines only 11Ib and 11II are above the average frequency, by 0.5% and 1.0%. 11Ia and 11III decrease by 1%, 11Ic by 4%, and 11Id by 1.5%. The frequency of 12I is only 0.5%, 2.5% below the average, and there are no 12II lines. With the exception of 13c, all types of 13-syllable lines increase in frequency, 13a by 2%, 13b by 10%, and 13d by 8.5%. 13c lines decrease 4.5%.

The number of 13-syllable lines in both *bylina* is above the average frequency, but there is a marked discrepancy between the frequencies of the line types which exhibit the increase. The difference between the two *bylina* in frequency of 13a lines is an increase of 15% in No. 74 and of only 2% in No. 77. In No. 77 lines 13b and 13d increase 10% and 8.5% respectively, while in No. 74 the frequency of 13b is only 0.5% above average and 13d is 1.5% below. This difference in frequency of line types may be due to frequent occurrence of a key word in No. 77, *poljanica*. This word in the middle of a 13-syllable line forms a 13b type line. Followed by a monosyllabic particle, it would form the second colon of a 13d line. As in subgroup 1, and especially in No. 78, the repetition of such words may create the rhythmic characteristics of the *bylina* in which they occur.

Subgroup 3. High frequency of 11-syllable lines. Nos. 75, 76, 82, and 83.

No. 75. "Il'ja Muromec i Kalin Car'". The frequency of 9-syllable lines is 7%, higher than in any other *bylina*. 10-syllable lines do not occur. The percentage of 11-syllable lines increases by 8%. 12-syllable lines decrease 4.0%. The greatest change in frequency is the 15% decrease in 13-syllable lines, from the average of 51% to 36%. 15-syllable lines increase 6%, and 17-syllable lines decrease by 1%.

All the line types of 11I and 11II show approximately the same increase in frequency, from 1.5% to 2.5%, so that the relationship between frequency of line types is the same as in the average curve. That is, 11Ia lines are more numerous than 11Ib, and 11Ic lines more than 11Id. The frequency of both 11III and 12I decrease by 1.5%, and 12II lines do not occur. All 13-syllable lines decrease, 13a and 13b by 3%; 13c most of all, by 6.5%; and 13d by 2.5%.

No. 76. "Il'ja Muromec v Ssore so Vladimirom". The frequency of 9-syllable lines is 2% above the average. Lines of ten syllables do not occur. Lines containing eleven syllables are 12% more frequent than the average. The frequencies of all the other lines are lower than the expected ones. The greatest decrease, 5%, is in 12-syllable lines. 13-syllable lines are 3% below average, 15-syllable lines 1% and 17-syllable 2%.

There is an increase in the total number, but not of all types, of 11-syllable lines. 11Ia lines show the greatest increase, 6.5%. The frequency of 11Ib is 2% above the average and is higher than the frequency of 11Ic, which is the same as the average. 11Ic lines are normally more numerous than 11Ib. The percentage of 11Id is 1% and 11II 2.5% higher than the average. 11III lines decrease by 0.5%. The frequency of 12I lines is 1%, 2% low. There are no 12II lines. The total number of 13-syllable lines decreases, but there is a 6.5% increase in 13a lines. There are 4.5% fewer 13b lines and 6% fewer 13c. There is no difference in the frequency of 13d.

No. 82. "Mixajlo Potyk". There are no 9-, 10-, 12-, and 17-syllable lines. 11-syllable lines are 9% over the average and 13-syllable 7%. The frequency of 15-syllable lines is 2% low.

There is a great increase in 11Ia lines, 7%. There is a smaller increase, 4.5%, in 11Ib lines. 11Ic lines decrease 4%, so that 11Ib lines are more numerous. The percentages of 11Id and 11II are high, by 1.5% and

2.5%, respectively. 11III and 12-syllable lines do not appear. The occurrence of 13a lines is very high, 27.5%, which is 8.5% above the average. Both 13b and 13d lines decrease, 13b by 0.5% and 13d by 4%. There is a 2% increase in 13c lines.

No. 83 "Ivan Godinovič". 9-syllable lines are 1% more frequent than the average. 10- and 12-syllable lines do not occur. The frequency of 11-syllable lines is 44%, 13% above average, and the highest in all the *bylina*. The frequency of 13-syllable lines is 6% low. Lines of 15-syllables decrease 3%. There is no change in the 17-syllable lines.

Despite the higher percentage of 11-syllable lines, 11Ia lines decrease by 0.5% and 11III by 2%. All the other 11-syllable lines increase. 11Ib is high by 3.5% and is higher than 11Ic, which is only 1% above average. 11Id lines are high by 2.5%. The greatest increase is in the number of 11II lines, 8.5%. 13a lines increase 3%. Other 13-syllable lines decrease, 13b by 4%, 13c by 2%, and 13d by 2.5%.

The percentage of 9-syllable lines in Nos. 75, 76, and 83 is higher than in other *bylina*, with the exception of No. 73 in group B. However, many 9-syllable lines in No. 73 differ from the ordinary ones by having a third unstressed syllable in the ending. None of the four *bylina* contains 10-syllable lines. Nos. 76, 82, and 83 are rhythmically more similar to each other than either is to No. 75. In No. 75 the increased frequency of the 11-syllable line types is approximately the same for all types, and all 13-syllable lines decrease. In Nos. 76, 82, and 83 the frequency of 11Ib is higher than 11Ic, the opposite of the normal distribution. These three have a higher than average frequency of 13a lines. 11II lines in all four *bylina* are noticeably more frequent.

2.4. *Group B. Lines with High Frequency of 12-Syllable Lines*

Nos. 73, 81, and 84.

No. 73. "Vol'ga i Mikula". The number of 9-syllable lines is 4% above average. The frequency of 10-syllable lines has increased even more, by 9%. Lines of 11-syllables are 2% high. The increase of 12-syllable lines is 19%. There is a great decrease in 13-syllable lines, 30%. There are no 15- or 17-syllable lines.

Although the total percentage of 11-syllable lines is above average, there are few 11I and 11III lines. 11Ia has the highest frequency but is still 5.5% lower than the average. There are no 11Ib and 11Id lines. 11Ic is 5% and 11II 4% less frequent. The most striking feature is the extremely high frequency of 11III lines, which rises 25% above average to 27.5%. Both types of 12-syllable lines have increased in frequency, 12I by 6% and 12II by 14%. 13a drops 15% and 13b 6.5%. The most frequent 13-syllable line is 13c, at 11.5%, which is a decrease of 6.5%; 13d lines decrease 2.5%.

In over one-third of the lines in this *bylina* three unstressed syllables instead of the usual two follow the last stress. This ending occurs most frequently in 11III lines, where almost half the lines end in this way. It is also very frequent in 12II lines. The last stressed syllable in both of these line types is preceded by two unstressed syllables. The appearance of the expanded endings in these lines could be a result of the extension of the rhythm of a preceding part of the line into the ending.

No. 81. "Dunaj". Lines with even numbers of syllables increase, those with odd numbers decrease. 9-syllable lines are 1% below average. The frequency of 11-syllable lines is 10% below the average. 13-syllable lines decrease by 12%. Lines of 15-syllables are 3% low. There are no 17-syllable lines. There is a 7% increase in 10-syllable lines and a 21% increase in 12-syllable lines.

Except for 11Ic, 11I and 11II lines are below average. The frequency of 11Ic is the same as the average. 11Ia decreases by 3.5% so that 11Ic is the most frequent 11I line, a reversal of the normal pattern. Lines 11Ib and 11Id both drop to 1.5%, a decrease of 4% and 2%. 11II lines are 4.5% lower than average. In contrast to other 11-syllable lines 11III increases 4%. The greatest increase is in the number of 12-syllable lines, 10% in 12I and 11.5% in 12II. All types of 13-syllable lines decrease. 13a, which is usually the most numerous, drops 5.5%, while 13c drops 2.5%. The result is that 13c lines are more frequent. Lines 13b and 13d have frequencies which are respectively 3% and 1% low.

No. 84. "Xoten Bludovič". There is a 1% decrease in 9-syllable lines. The decrease is 5% in 11-syllable and 22% in 13-syllable lines. Lines of 15- and 17-syllables do not occur. The rise in frequency of 10-syllable lines is 1.5%. The 33% increase in 12-syllable lines is the highest observed.

11Ia lines decrease 5%, 11Ib 4.5%. The only type of 11I line to increase is 11Ic. The rise is 5%, which makes it the most frequent 11-syllable line. The drop in frequency of 11Id is 2%. No 11II lines appear. The frequency of 11III rises 6.5%. 12I lines are the most numerous, 24%, which is an increase of 21%. The increase in 12II lines is less, 12.5%. All types of 13-syllable lines decrease. 13a decreases most, by 8.5%, 13b by 5%, 13c by 6%, and 13d by 3.5%.

The outstanding feature of the group is the large number of 12-syllable lines. They are the most frequent types in No. 84, but the 11-syllable line is more frequent in No. 73 and the 13-syllable in No. 81. Of the 12-syllable lines, 12II is more frequent than 12I in Nos. 73 and 81, but not in No. 84. 11III lines are usually the least frequent of the 11-syllable lines, but in this group they are among the most frequent lines containing eleven syllables. They occur in No. 73 more frequently than any other line type. 11Ic lines are the most frequent 11I lines, except in No. 73 where very few lines of the 11I type occur. Among the 13-syllable types 13c is the most numerous. Thus, the appearance of high frequency of 12-syllable lines is accompanied by high frequencies of some line types with odd numbers of syllables so that such line types are the most frequent of those with the same number of syllables.

There is a sequence of two unstressed syllables between the first two stresses of 12I lines and between the last two stresses of 12II. In 11III lines this is the only sequence which appears. The increase in these line types is related to this sequence of unstressed syllables. The common feature shared by the 11- and 13-syllable line types which show an increase in frequency is the construction of the second colon, which in both ends in two unstressed syllables, –/– –. In 12I lines a second colon having this form is the most frequent, in contrast to all other lines, except 17-syllable, which have the final stresses separated by three unstressed syllables. Thus, the most frequent lines of these *bylina* are those possessing sequences of two unstressed syllables between stresses and also two unstressed syllables after the stress of a colon. In No. 73 the frequency of 11III and 12-syllable lines is sufficiently high that its meter must be recognized as different from the meter of the *bylina* in group A, since over half of the lines are of these types. In Nos. 81 and 84 these lines make up approximately one-third of the lines and modify the overall metrical contour but are not numerous enough to shift the *bylina* into a different meter.

The occurrence of these lines cannot be due to mistakes on the part of the performer, since they are found almost exclusively in the three *bylina*. Moreover, in a Petersburg performance Rjabinin transferred "Dunaj" from its usual "dactylic" meter to the normal "trochaic" one of other *bylina*. He explained that he was tired and that the real meter was too difficult. Therefore, he recited "Dunaj" in an easier meter. When Gil'ferding requested that he repeat "Dunaj" in this meter for recording, Rjabinin refused, saying that it would not be the proper form for "Dunaj". The difference in meter and rhythm between "Dunaj" and other *bylina* must have been a real one for Rjabinin.

In discussing Rybnikov's comment that Rjabinin sang "Staver", "Vol'ga i Mikula", and "Mixajlo Potyk" to the same melody and that each *bylina* created a different impression, Gil'ferding observed that the basis of the melody is the meter of the verse.[2] If the melody of "Vol'ga i Mikula" and "Mixajlo Potyk" was the same, the melody cannot be the explanation for the differences in meter of the two *bylina*. They are the extremes of the two metrical tendencies observed in Rjabinin's *bylina*. Whereas 11III and 12-syllable lines are the most common in "Vol'ga i Mikula", none occurs in "Mixajlo Potyk". Lines 11Ia, 13a, and 13c are considerably above the average frequency in "Mixajlo Potyk" but decrease in "Vol'ga i Mikula". Whatever the relationship between verse meter and melody, differences of melody cannot account for the metrical and rhythmical characteristics of the two *bylina*.

[2]   A. F. Gil'ferding, *Onežskie byliny*, 4th ed. (Moscow-Leningrad, 1949), I, p. 66.

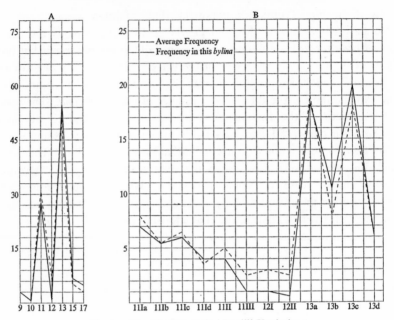

Fig. 1.   No. 80, Dobrynja i Vasilij Kazimirov

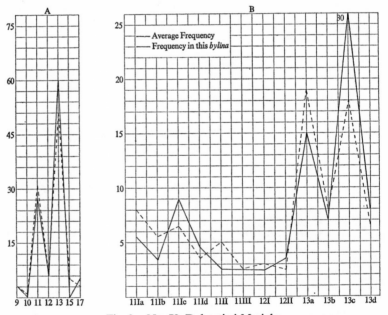

Fig. 2.   No. 78, Dobrynja i Marinka

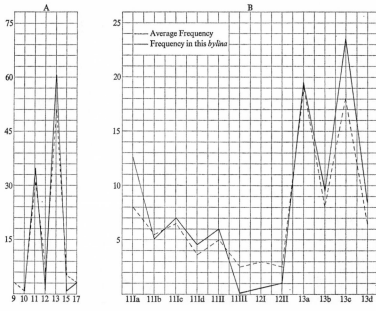

Fig. 3. No. 79, Dobrynja i Zmej

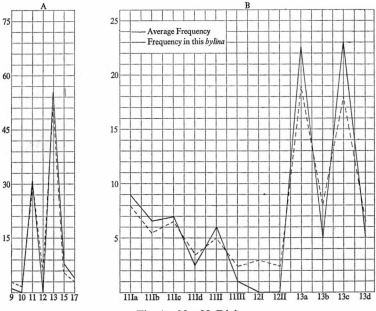

Fig. 4. No. 85, Djuk

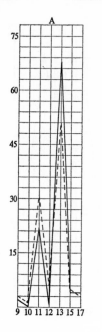

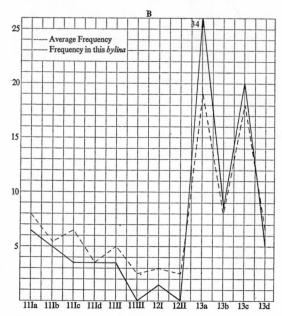

Fig. 5.   No. 74, Il'ja i Solovej

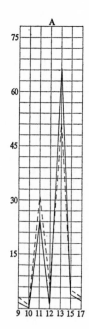

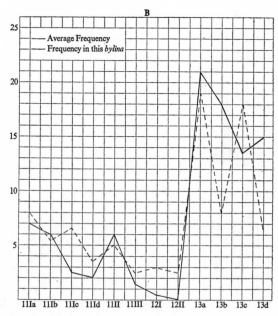

Fig. 6.   No. 77, Il'ja Muromec i Doč' ego

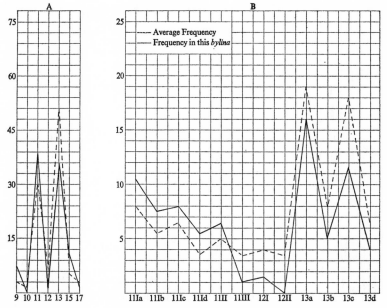

Fig. 7. No. 75, Il'ja Muromec i Kalin Car' the average curve for 11III, 12I+12II
is 1°/₀ high

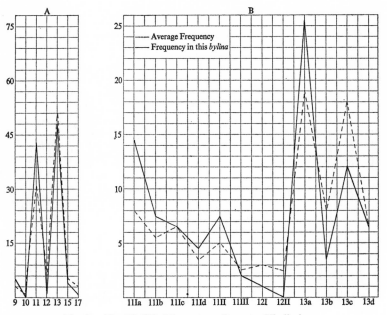

Fig. 8. No. 76, Il'ja Muromec v Ssore so Vladimirom

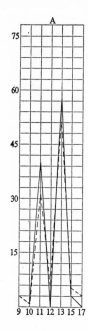
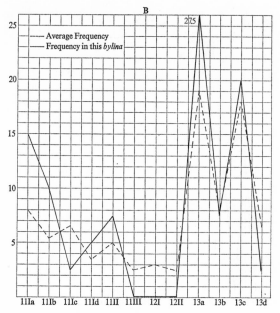

Fig. 9. No. 82, Mixajlo Potyk

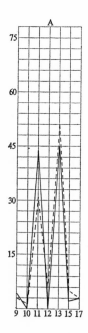
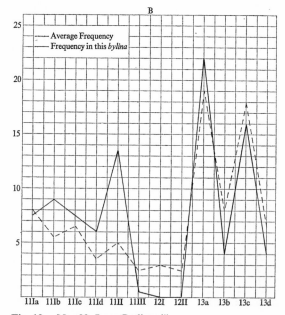

Fig. 10. No. 83, Ivan Godinovič

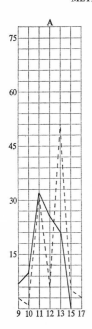
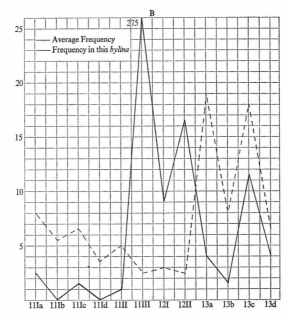

Fig. 11. No. 73, Vol'ga i Mikula

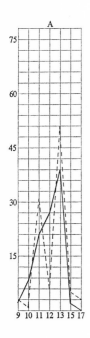
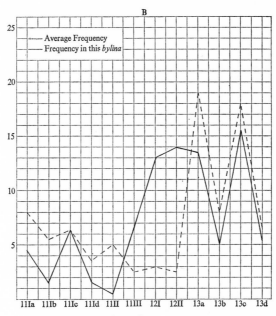

Fig. 12. No. 81, Dunaj

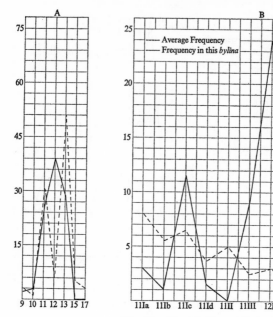

Fig. 13.   No. 84, Xoten Bludovič

V

REPETITION OF PREPOSITIONS

1. INTRODUCTION

A striking feature of the language of the *bylina* is the frequent repetition of prepositions. The following examples are typical.

Iz togo li-to *iz* goroda *iz* Muromlja	74,1
A *u* slavnogo *u* knjaz'ja *u* Vladyrmira	75,6
Ešče *v* tret'ii podkopy *vo* glubokii	75,391
Da j *na* svoj *na* slavnyj *na* širok *na* dvor	79,39

Prepositions may be repeated before all members of a phrase or before only some of them. On the other hand, it is not unusual for a preposition not to be repeated.

Porozgnevalsja *na* starogo kazaka Il'ju Muromca	75,2
A on edet-to *po* slavnomu čistu polju	74,134
Vy postojte-tko *za* slavnyj stol'nij Kiev grad	75,276

Since most prepositions comprise syllables, their repetition or lack of it could be a factor in the patterning of stressed and unstressed syllables. To establish the existence of a purely stylistic function of repetition, the usage in *bylina* must be compared with occurrences of repetition in non-poetic language.

2. EXTENT OF REPETITION

Repetition of prepositions is found not only in folk poetry but also in Old Church Slavic and Old Russian texts.

2.1. *Repetition in Old Russian*

The most extensive conditions for repetition in the old language are given by Bulaxovskij.[1]

---

[1] L. A. Bulaxovskij, *Istoričeskij kommentarij k russkomu jazyku* (Kiev, 1958), p. 344.

1. Before a word in apposition.
2. Before an adjective following a noun.
3. Before a noun preceded by an adjective. (Rarer).
4. Before the second of two adjectives preceding a noun. (Rarer).
5. In numerals.

2.2 Repetition in the Dialects

Mansikka describes repetition before each word in a phrase as being constant in the *Šenkurskaja uezda*.[2] When materials were collected thirty or forty years later for the *Dialect Atlas of the Russian Language* in the areas which Mansikka studied, it was found that repetition was a sporadic phenomenon even in the speech of the oldest generation.[3] It seems unlikely that if repetition were as regular as Mansikka described it, that it should have become sporadic in so short a time. Evgen'eva states that the material for the dialect atlas collected in 1937-1939 in different parts of the Karelian Autonomous Republic, the southeastern parts of the *Arxangelskaja Oblast'*, and the northern regions of the *Vologodskaja Oblast'* revealed that prepositions were repeated, though sporadically, under the following conditions:[4]

1. When an attribute follows the word it modifies.
2. When an attribute precedes the word it modifies.
   (All examples quoted are repetitions after pronouns. R.J.).
3. Before words in apposition.
4. In complex numerals.

2.3. *Repetition in* Bylina

From the examples quoted earlier it is seen that in the *bylina* a preposition may be repeated before one, some, or none of the words in a phrase. Štokmar considers repetition to be one of the important factors which contributes to the "mnogosložnost'" of the folk language; that is, in his view to the greater proportion of unstressed to stressed syllables than is found in the literary language.[5] He does not state under what

[2] Mansikka, "O govore Šenkurskogo uezda Arxangel'skoj gubernii", *Izvestija Otdelenija russkogo jazyka i slovestnosti*, Vol. XVII, Book 2 (St. Petersburg, 1912), p. 142.
[3] A. P. Evgen'eva, *Očerki po jazyku russkoj ustnoj poèzii v zapisjax XVII-XX vv* (Moscow-Leningrad, 1963), p. 48.
[4] Evgen'eva, *ibid.*, p. 53.
[5] M. P. Štokmar, *Issledovanija v oblasti russkogo narodnogo stixosloženija* (Moscow, 1952), p. 277.

conditions prepositions are repeated. In her study of repetition of prepositions in *bylina* of the northern tradition recorded in the nineteenth
century, Evgen'eva gives the following environments in which prepositions are repeated.[6]

1. When an attribute follows the word it modifies.
2. When an attribute precedes the word it modifies.
3. When there are several attributes which both precede and follow
    the word they modify.
4. In appositions.

Except for repetition in complex numerals, the conditions given for
repetition in certain Old Russian texts, the dialects and *bylina* are essentially the same. Repetition in phrases containing adjectives may
generally occur whatever the position of the adjective with regard to
the noun it modifies. Mansikka's description of repetition in the dialects
is more similar to Evgen'eva's description of repetition in nineteenth
century *bylina* than it is to her findings for the dialects, if her second
condition for the dialects is understood to apply only to pronouns. She
concludes that Mansikka probably simplified somewhat the situation
when he stated that the norm for the use of prepositions in the dialects
was obligatory repetition before each word in agreement.[7] However,
she identifies the kind of repetition Mansikka found in dialects with
that in the *bylina* recorded by Gil'ferding and Rybnikov in the statement that:

It may be said with complete confidence that the repetition of prepositions
in the form that V. Mansikka described it, and as it is found in the *bylina*
recorded by Rybnikov and Gil'ferding has disappeared from living use.[8]

Thus, the norm in Rjabinin's dialect, or at least in his *bylina*, should be
constant repetition. Constant repetition is not observed in his *bylina*,
but neither is it sporadic as in the modern dialects.

Evgen'eva rejects a stylistic basis for the kind of repetition found in
Rjabinin's *bylina*, observing that the prepositions *v*, *k*, and *s*, are very
often repeated and cannot affect the meter.[9] However, it is precisely
the repetition of these forms of the prepositions which can indicate
what the linguistic norm was in Rjabinin's dialect.

[6] Evgen'eva, *op. cit.*, p. 47ff.
[7] *Ibid.*, p. 48.
[8] *Ibid.*, p. 53.
[9] *Ibid.*, p. 47.

The determination of whether or not repetition plays a metrical role in *bylina* is complicated by the fact that, since most prepositions are of at least one syllable and all may be, it is unavoidable that they affect the metrical structure whatever the reason for their repetition. In the absence of non-literary texts, only when there is no possibility that a preposition has been repeated in *bylina* for metrical purposes can it be used with any assurance as an example in the determination of the linguistic rule requiring repetition.

3. SYNTACTIC BASIS OF REPETITION

The only prepositions whose repetition cannot influence the meter are *v*, *k*, and *s* in the consonantal forms. It may be expected that the repetition of even these forms will not always follow exact rules, since dialect studies show that there is no longer a consistent usage in everyday language, where the question of metrical requirements cannot arise. Inconsistency in usage could be compounded in *bylina* if repetition has a metrical function, for repetition for this purpose would lead to an even greater weakening of the observance of the linguistic rule.

In the thirteen *bylina* comprising the text of this study, the consonantal forms *v*, *k*, and *s* occur 150 times as repeated prepositions within prepositional phrases. The conditions for repetition are given below.

	Position	%
1.	Before an adjective following a noun.	38
2.	Before a word in apposition.	34
3.	Before a pronoun after a noun.	1
4.	After a pronoun before a noun.	14
5.	After an adjective before a noun.	13

There are 21 phrases in which the members are separated from each other by other words, mainly by particles. They are all of types 1, 2, or 3. Since repetition would be expected whether or not the members of the phrase were separated, no new category has been set up. Examples of the four groups follow.

1. Repetition before an adjective following a noun:

Prixodil en *vo* konjušen'ku *v* stojaluju	79,340
Priudarit' nado *v* kop'ja *v* muržameckii	77,159
Podxodi-ko ty *ko* stoliku *k* dubovomu	75,47
Da *k* tomu kolečiku *k* serebrjanu	80,702

* Apposition may be too restrictive a term to describe the relationship between some pairs of nouns.

Da *so* vseju svoej sily *s* bogatyrskoju 77,147
Da iz toju li *so* Galiči *s* prokljatoju 85,1

2. Repetition before a word in apposition:

Gde nam s"exat'sja *v* rozdol'ice *v* čistom poli 80,140
B'et nogamy *v* matušku *v* syru zemlju 77,326
Podxodila-to *ko* staromu kazake *k* Il'e Muromcu 77,185
K korolju-to *k* Botijanu Botijanovu 80,16
Poroz"exat'sja *s* rozdol'ica *s* čista polja 77,157
Vyxodili ony *s* matuški *s* bož'ej cerkvy 82,53

3. Repetition before a pronoun after a noun:

Vo dospexi on da *v* svoi krepkii 79,392
A j pošlo-to *ko* Dobrynjuške tatar *k* nemu desjatkami 80,588

4. Repetition after a pronoun before a noun:

Da *vo* èty *v* strelku *vo* kalenuju 78,45
Da j *vo* našem *v* slavnom Volyn-gorode 85,118
Da *ko* tem *k* gorodam za polučkoju 73,79
I priveli *k* tobe *k* sobake carju Kalinu 75,461
A *so* toju *s* Nastas'ej korolevičnoj 81,326
So svoej *s* družinuški s xorobroej 73,103

Nineteen cases of repetition cannot be assigned to any of the preceding groups. The preposition is repeated after an adjective which precedes a noun. However, such repetition is confined to a few phrases. Prepositions are repeated after the word *slavnyj* nine times, after *molodoj* before *Dobrynuška* three times, after *bogatyj* in four repetitions of the same line, and once after *belyj*, *staryj*, and *tatarskij*.

5. Repetition after specific adjectives before nouns:

a. After *slavnyj*:
Aj *vo* slavnoe *v* rozdol'ice čisto pole 77,162
Podošla by ty *ko* slavnomu *k* Kijan-morju 80,179

b. After *molodoj*:
Podnosili-to *k* molodomu *k* Dobrynjuške 80,465

c. After *bogatyj*:
Da j *vo* slavnoem bogatom *v* Volyn-gorode 85,180
Da *so* slavnogo bogata *s* Volyn-goroda 85,95

    d. After *belyj*:

        Vo svoi beret *vo* belye *v* ručuški   78,41

    e. After *tatarskij*:

        Ne xodi tol'ko *v* tatarskuju *v* slobodušku   78,14

Some 72% of the repetitions occur when an adjective follows its noun and before a noun in apposition. Repetition after a pronoun preceding a noun accounts for 14% of the occurrences. This type of repetition is explicitly stated as a conditioning factor only by Evgen'eva in her study of *bylina* of the seventeenth and eighteenth centuries, and then only after *ves'* and *vsjakij*.[10] Repetition occurs in the *bylina* of Rjabinin after personal, demonstrative, and possessive pronouns. The reason for repetition under these conditions may be similar to that for repetition before words in apposition. That is, the relationship between a pronoun, especially personal and demonstrative, and the noun it modifies could be similar to the relationship between two nouns in apposition, thus requiring repetition. The following examples are typical. The pronoun occurs after the noun in the first example, before it in the second.

    A j pošlo-to *ko* Dobrynjuške tatar *k* nemu desjatkami   80,588

    I preveli *k* tobe *k* sobake carju Kalinu   75,461

The similarity between the usage of pronouns and adjectives could contribute to the repetition of prepositions after adjectives preceding nouns by analogy to the pronoun, where repetition is observed whatever the position of the pronoun.

    The infrequency of repetition after adjectives before nouns and the fact that such repetitions are restricted to only six adjectives is insufficient evidence to suggest that the norm in Rjabinin's dialect could have been repetition of the preposition before each word in a phrase, as Mansikka states in his dialect studies and as Efgen'eva suggests in her study of the language of *bylina* recorded by Rybnikov and Gil'ferding.

    Inconsistency in repetition is observed even in the early texts, so it is not surprising that there are apparent deviations in Rjabinin's usage. Whatever the norm for repetition was in Rjabinin's dialect, the conditions exemplified by the prepositions *v*, *k*, and *s* must approximate that norm. Rjabinin repeats these prepositions in specific environments, but not in every occurrence of these environments. Prepositions may or may not be repeated. If they are repeated, it is in these environments.

---

[10] *Ibid.*, p. 42.

Significant deviation from this norm in repetition of other prepositions in Rjabinin's *bylina* must be dependent on metrical requirements.

4. REPETITION AS A METRICAL DEVICE

It can be assumed that the repetition of the consonantal forms of *v*, *k*, and *s* is determined by the same language rules which condition repetition of prepositions which make up a syllable. Therefore, prepositions which are syllables should follow the rules established for *v*, *k*, and *s*, where the only conditioning factor is the requirement of the language. It has been shown that in a *bylina* line the stressed and unstressed syllables are arranged in a definite relationship to each other, so that in a thirteen-syllable line there are always three unstressed syllables between two stressed ones, and in an 11I line the first two stressed syllables are separated by one unstressed syllable and the last two by three. 75% of the lines in the text are of these types. Thus in the *bylina* there arises the possibility of conflict between the rules for repeating prepositions and the requirements of the meter. Metrical requirements take precedence in such instances, for no examples are found where the meter is broken by the repetition of a preposition. In this and the following chapters "meter" and "metrical requirements" refer to the distribution of all stresses in Groups 1 and 3 as well as to the clear tendency for stresses in the other groups to be separated by an odd number of syllables.

4.1. *Repetition of Variants of V, K, and S*

The sequence of three unstressed syllables required by the meter is attained in the first of the following lines by the particle *da*, which is followed by the consonantal form of the preposition. The particle does not appear in the second line, and the preposition has its non-consonantal form.

Priezžal on ko gorám da *k* soročínskiem	79,61
Da j ko tym gorám *ko* soročínskiem	79,53

The following examples show clearly that the meter is the reason for *v* in the first example having its consonantal form, for the appearance of its non-consonantal form in the second, and for *po*, which may have only this form, not being repeated in the third example.

Da j sidit ona vo téremi *v* zlatóm verxu	81,46
On prixodit-to vo térem *vo* zlatý verxi	81,110

Po tomu-to téremu ___ zlatú verxu   81,111

The same expression terminates the three lines, but its grammatical form is different in each. There is one unstressed syllable before its stress, the last in the line. The word preceding the expression is the same in all lines, but the number of syllables in it is not the same because of case differences. In the first example two unstressed syllables follow the second stress of the line and with the syllable before the final stress comprise a 3-syllable sequence. Therefore, the preposition must have its consonantal form. However, only one unstressed syllable follows the second stress in the second example. The preposition takes the non-consonantal form and supplies the syllable needed for a 3-syllable sequence. The preposition *po* has no consonantal alternant. Its repetition in the third example would create a sequence of four unstressed syllables. Consequently, Rjabinin does not repeat it.

4.2. *Prepositions without Consonantal Forms*

The prepositions in the following lines must consist of one syllable. When repetition would produce a metrically unpermitted sequence, the preposition is not repeated. Rjabinin consistently avoids repeating a preposition if it would interrupt the meter. The conditions for repetition as determined by the occurrence of *v*, *k*, and *s* are found in the lines. In the first of two lines compared the preposition is repeated, in the second it is not.

1. Repetition before an adjective following a noun:

Mog by postojat' odin *za* cérkvi *za* sobórnyi	75,14
Zavodil ego *za* stóliki ___ dubóvyi	75,137
Na dobróm koni *na* bogatýrskoem	77,51
Priezžal *na* zástavu ___ moskóvskuju	77,59
Kak *ot* pókriku *ot* čelovéč'jago	75,196
I *ot* negó li-to *ot* pósvistu ___ solóv'jago	74,43

2. Repetition before words in apposition:

Da postoj-ko ty *za* knjázja *za* Vladýmira	75,149
Da ne budem my stojat' *za* mátuški ___ bož'í cerkvi	75,288
En *po* górodu *po* Kíevu poxažívat	76,29
To idet on *po* rozdól'icu ___ čistú polju	75,510
Da *u* slavnago *u* knjázja *u* Vladýmira	75,38
Nagnano *u* sobáki ___ carja Kálina	75,376

3. Repetition after pronouns before nouns:

Za togó *za* sýna-to za car'skogo	83,42
Za togó ___ Oléšen'ku Popoviča	80,997
Ot togó *ot* pósvistu solov'jago	85,344
A *ot* tój ___ pšený ot belojarovoj	75,357

Although repetition of prepositions has its origin in the language itself, it is clear from these examples that the predominant factor in determining the repetition in *bylina* is not a language rule but the meter.

Appositional constructions and the occurrence of adjectives after the noun they modify are very frequent in *bylina*. The language thus provides the basis for repetition in these cases. Since fluctuation in the repetition is seen as early as Old Russian texts, it is highly unlikely that Rjabinin strictly observed the rules in his native dialect. Although repetition is allowed by the syntax in some constructions, prepositions are not consistently repeated even when the conditioning factors are present, so prepositions which could have been repeated can be omitted to meet the metrical requirements. The next step of repeating the preposition in any phrase for metrical reasons alone is one easily taken. The repetition of prepositions where syntax does not permit it, e.g., when an adjective precedes its noun, shows that meter and not syntax has become the determining factor and that repetition in such cases has acquired a metrical function.

Da [na] malyx perelétnyix *na* séryx utušek	75,362
To on den' edet po krásnomu *po* sólnyšku	79,59
Da j ko láskovu *ko* knjázju na širok na dvor	85,68

VI

MORPHOLOGICAL VARIANTS AND METRICAL ALTERNANTS

1. INTRODUCTION

Morphological features from various stages in the development of Russian have been preserved in the *bylina*. Both ancient and modern forms may coexist or a feature lost in the modern language may survive in the *bylina*. There is no difference in meaning in the coexisting forms. One of the alternants usually contains one syllable more than the other. The performers of *bylina* have recognized the metrical significance of this alternation in number of syllables of the same form, and the appearance of one or the other is primarily metrically determined.

2. ALTERNATION OF LONG AND SHORT ENDINGS OF ADJECTIVES AND PRONOUNS

There were two adjective declensions in Old Russian, the definite and indefinite. The indefinite declension was identical with one of the nominal declensions. The definite adjectives were formed by adding enclitic pronouns to the indefinite forms. Both types were fully declined and could have either a predicative or attributive function and could precede or follow the noun with which they were in agreement. In modern Russian the short indefinite adjectives are indeclinable, changing their form only for gender in the singular and having a single plural form. They may function only as predicatives. The endings of some of the definite adjectives in the modern language are shorter by one syllable than the endings in Old Russian, through the contraction of vowels. Adjectives in *bylina* may have endings which correspond to the indefinite declension, to the old uncontracted forms of the definite declension, at least in number of syllables whether or not they are the same vowels or their reflexes, or endings which correspond to those of the contemporary language.

The forms of both the definite and indefinite declensions have been retained, but the distinction in meaning has been lost. As the semantic distinction was being lost, the definite and indefinite forms could have been used interchangeably. Their usage could then be conditioned by other factors. Conforming to a definite metrical scheme could result in the narrator selecting the long or the short form as the meter demanded. The adjective endings then would become one of the means by which the requirements of the meter are met. The examples below show that the occurrence of a particular adjective ending is determined by the meter.

2.1. *Adjectives within the Line*

In these lines the adjective and the noun it modifies are stressed on the first syllable. The adjective has the contracted ending in the first example so that three syllables separate the two main stresses. In the second example the disyllabic ending and the preposition form a sequence of three unstressed syllables. The omission of either would form a sequence of two unstressed syllables, which is not permitted. In the last example the pronoun *on* replaces the additional syllable of the disyllabic ending and with the preposition makes up the required three-syllable sequence.

Ne slučilosja *ničtó byt' v belyx rúčuškax*	79,146
Emu ničego vzjat' *v bélyi vo rúčuški*	79,151
Vo svoi beret *vo bély on vo ručuški*	74,80

The alternation in the following lines is the same as that in the first two of the preceding lines.

Da on *stál u dobryx mólodcev* vysprašivat'	80,403
Stal korol' *u dóbryix u mólodcev* vysprašivat'	80,383

The following examples illustrate the alternation of prepositions and the endings of the definite adjectives with the uncontracted adjective endings so that a three syllable sequence between stresses is obtained. If the preposition were not repeated in one line and the uncontracted ending not used in the other, there would be an unpermitted sequence of two syllables. If the ending were the uncontracted one and the preposition repeated in the same line, four syllables would separate the stressed syllable, which is also not permitted by the meter.

Na vsix sil'nix rus'skiix *mogúčix na bogátyrej*	80,4
Slavynx sil'nyix *mogúčiix bogátyrej*	76,4

Ko tym *slávnym ko gorám* da k soročinskiim   74,311
Ko tym *slávnyim gorám* da soročinskiim   74,224

The occurrence of the long or short form of the ending is determined by the position of the stress of the word which follows the adjective in the lines below. The adjective is stressed on the first syllable. The stress is on the third syllable of the noun in the first example. The single syllable of the short adjective ending gives the required sequence of three syllables. In the second example the noun is stressed on the second syllable. With the short ending the stressed syllable of the adjective is followed by one syllable, which would from with the noun a non-metrical sequence of two syllables. Therefore, the long ending is used and an acceptable sequence formed.

Da j vo *slávna Svjatogóra* vo bogatyrja   80,192
Da j vo *slávnago bogátyrja* v Olešen'ku Popoviča   80,194

The following lines contain the same adjective stressed on the second syllable. The noun in the first line is stressed on the first syllable so that the short ending gives a metrically acceptable sequence while the long one would not. The stress on the noun in the second line is on the second syllable, and the disyllabic ending provides the number of syllables which the meter requires. The short ending and a particle could have been used, as is shown in later examples.

To *velíki zápisi* nemalyi   79,173
Vse *velíkie dvorý* da knjaženeckii   75,56

The words after the adjectives have one unstressed syllable before the stress in the following examples. The adjectives are stressed on the syllable before the ending. A sequence of fewer than two syllables is impossible even by using the short ending. In the first example the two-syllable sequence is avoided by the appearance of a one-syllable pronoun after the adjective, in the second line by the use of the long ending.

Makovi on *zoločény vsi povýstreljal*   76,17
A vse makovki on *zoločényi povýstreljal*   76,32
Da ne *málu on stopú* da poltora vedra   74,247
Ty ne *máluju stopú* da poltora vedra   74,242

2.2. *Pronouns*

Possessive and demonstrative pronouns may also have extended endings. When the noun is stressed on the second syllable as in the first line below, the pronoun has the regular ending so that the stresses are separated by one syllable. With the noun stressed on the first syllable, the extended ending appears and forms the same sequence.

Da *ko tým zverjám* ko poedučiim	85,52
Da *ko týim zméjam* poklevučiim	85,42

In both of the following lines the words following the pronouns are stressed on the first syllable. With the regular pronominal ending there is one syllable between the two stresses. In the second example a three-syllable sequence is formed by the extended ending and by the use of the nonconsonantal form of the preposition.

Da j *vo nášem v slávnom* Volyn-gorode	85,118
Da j *vo nášoem vo górode* vo Kieve	85,544

2.3. *Adjectives at the End of the Line*

The place of the accent of an adjective determines the form of the ending when the adjective appears in final position in the line. If the last syllable of the adjective stem is stressed, the ending is disyllabic; if it is stressed on the penultimate syllable, the ending is monosyllabic.

The disyllabic endings of the adjectives stressed on the final stem syllable in the following lines form the dactylic ending.

On spustilsja s toj so gory so vysókii	75,209
A j u tyx li u šatrov u bélyix	75,522
J on prosel s konem da bogatýrskiim	75,419
Ne pobit' tobi toj siluški velíkii	75,375
Ty ostaneš'sja v podkopax vo glubókiix	75,394

The stress on the adjectives in final position in the following lines is on the penultimate syllable of the stem. The endings are monosyllabic.

On prišel v polatu belokámennu	74,139
A on bral-to svoj-ot tugoj luk rozrývčatoj	80,543
A j Vladymir knjaz' da stol'ni-kíevskoj	85,455
Il'ja Muromec da on trinádcatyj	75,256
Vyxodili mužički da tut černígovski	74,19

The following lines show the variation in the ending of an adjective with a diminutive suffix and of the same adjective without it. Rhythmically, the syllable of the diminutive suffix replaces one syllable of the long ending. The unsuffixed adjectives have the definite ending, the suffixed forms the indefinite ending.

J on spustil kak èty tetivočku šelkóvuju	75,541
Natjanul tetivočku šelkóven'ku	75,527
Ena estvušku postavit' da xoróšuju	75,22
En snarjadnuju odežicu xoróšen'ku	85,283

Vasil'ev observed that the uncontracted forms of adjective endings are usually found at the end of the line.[1] Jakobson states that their appearance in this position is supported by metrical demands.[2] It has been shown that the uncontracted forms occur also within the line, where their alternation with the contracted forms is one of the chief means of meeting metrical requirements. The variety of ways in which they are used indicates that they are not merely preservations in fixed expressions or in certain positions in the line, but are consciously interchanged with the definite and indefinite forms, depending on the rhythmical structure of the words with which they combine to make up a line.

The three types of adjective endings alternate so that metrically appropriate sequences of unstressed syllables result. The consistency in usage must be determined by the meter, for there is no semantic difference in the endings which could be the determining factor. The semantic difference between the definite and indefinite forms of the adjectives was lost. The formal difference, the number of syllables in the endings, has been retained and serves in *bylina* a purely rhythmical function. The uncontracted endings provide disyllabic alternants for the cases which contain only one syllable in the definite ending.

3. INFINITIVES

Infinitives which occur in the *bylina* have the endings -*t'* and stressed and unstressed -*ti*. -*t'* and stressed -*ti* (except certain prefixed verbs), occur in the literary language, but in the north Russian dialects infinitives in unstressed -*ti* have been preserved.[3] In the *bylina* of Rjabinin both -*t'* and unstressed -*ti* occur with the same verb stem. Since this

---

[1]   L. Vasil'ev, "Jazyk belomorskix bylin", *Izvestija Otdelenija russkogo jazyka i slovenosti*, Series 2, Vol. VII, Book 4 (1902), p. 33.
[2]   Roman Jakobson, "O sootnošenii meždu pesennoj i razgovornoj narodnoj reč'ju", *Voprosy jazykoznanija*, No. 3 (1962), p. 89.
[3]   L. A. Bulaxovskij, *Istoričeskij kommentarij k russkomu jazyku* (Kiev, 1958), p. 344.

alternation of the two endings with the same stem provides the means of expressing the same concept in different numbers of syllables, it is possible that the meter determines which form occurs. Vasil'ev notes that infinitives in -ti usually occur at the end of the line.[4] The position of the infinitives which occur in the bylina studied follows.

Type of Ending	Position	
	Non-final	Final
1. Stem-t'	236	51
2. Stem-yva-t'	2	68
3. Stem-yva-ti	—	13
4. Stem-ti (stressed -ti)	28	—
5. Stem-ti (unstressed -ti)	7	55

Some infinitive types occur only in non-final position while others are found only at the end of the line. Some occur in both positions, but are much more frequent in one than in the other. Only those infinitives which have a dactyl stress pattern may occur at the end of the line and make up the dactylic close. Twenty-two of the infinitives at line end in the first group are mono- or di-syllabic and cannot alone form the close. They may be rhythmically dependent on a preceding word which has the main stress. All except four of the twenty-two are of this type.

Knjazju-to Vladymiru da golová srubit'	75,30
Bož'i cerkvi vse na dým spustit'	75,272
Stal on silušku koném toptat'	75,367

There are three occurrences of podnját' nel'zja in which the infinitive has the main stress.

A im soški ot zemli podnját' nel'zja	73, 111, 122, 133

One example is a complex construction of two infinitives.

Da stal parobok dobra konja kormít' poit'	79,204

Although these infinitives occur at the line end, they form the close only in combination with other words. There are nine infinitives of this group which are stressed on the penultimate stem syllable and contain the suffix -sja, which helps to form the dactylic ending.

Čtoby bylo mne na čto da ponadéjat'sja	80,244
Emu nečem-to s tatarami da j poprotívit'sja	80,605

One infinitive has the suffix -ova.

4 Vasil'ev, op. cit., p. 33.

Mni-ka nadobno Bož'ja pomoč' krest'jánovat'	73,55

The remaining examples in the first group are disyllabic stems with a stressed prefix, most frequently *vy-*.

Da ne iz čego bogatyrju povýstrelit'	80,498
Černed' mužikov on vsex povýrubit'	75,271
Skoro ždat' velit nam, kogdy dóžidat'	80,264

All the examples in the third group (*-yva-ti*) are found in "Dunaj", "Vol'ga i Mikula", and "Xoten Bludovič". As has already been pointed out, some lines in these *bylina* have sequences of two unstressed syllables between stressed syllables. Gil'ferding often marked a second stress on the final syllable of these infinitives, representing a melodic accent. The result is a sequence of two unstressed syllables which continues the internal rhythm of the line and replaces the usual dactylic ending. Since the forms occur only in these *bylina* they indicate a variation in the line end under the influence of the "anapestic" tendency of the internal rhythm. All the other infinitives in *-yva-* have the *-t'* suffix (the second group), and with the exception of two examples are in final position. The syllable before the *-yva-* suffix is stressed, which gives a dactylic ending.

Almost 90 percent of the infinitives in *-ti*, the fifth group, occur at the end of the line. The stress is on the penultimate stem syllable, and the *-ti* suffix provides the additional syllable needed for the dactylic ending. Since unstressed *-ti* occurs in these *bylina* almost exclusively in the final position, it must occur for the sake of meter. The following examples illustrate the occurrence of one and the same verb with *-ti* at the end of the line but with *-t'* within the line. Non-metrical sequences of syllables would be formed if the infinitives within the line had the *-ti* ending, while the infinitive with the *-t'* ending would not form the dactylic ending of the line.

Nam kuda veliš' itti da j kudy *éxati*	77,96
Komu *éxat'* nam v rozdol'ice čisto pole	77,24
A'šče znaju ja kogo poslat' *poéxati*	80,32
Im *poéxat'* nadobno k obedenke xristovskoju	85,280
Poxotel-to on da *poženítisja*	83,2
Xočeš' exat' *poženít'sja* v Zolotu ordu	83,7
Pošel siluški velikoj u tatar da *pootvédati*	80,569
Pootvédat' nado siluški velikoju	77,25

Any infinitive with a dactylic stress pattern can theoretically form the close. Actually, only four types occur. Two types are fairly infrequent, infinitives with -*sja* and those in which the stress is on a prefix. Infinitives in -*yva*- and unstressed -*ti* comprise almost two-thirds of the number occurring at the end of the line. Their almost exclusive use at the end of the line shows that the infinitive ending in unstressed -*ti* is a metrical device to obtain the dactylic close and that the occurrence of -*yva*- infinitives in this position is conditioned by the meter.

4. LOSS OF *j* AND VOWEL CONTRACTION

One of the features peculiar to North Russian dialects is the loss of intervocalic *j* and subsequent vowel contraction. Such contraction has occurred in some personal forms of the verbs in Rjabinin's *bylina*. Only uncontracted forms of verbs are found at the beginning of the line.

Pod"ezžaet on ko rečke ko Smorodinki	74,57
Otsylaet ko sobake carju Kalinu	75,90
Dožidaet krestnička ljubimago	83,173

Even verbs with the -*yvaj* suffix, which are the ones most often having the contracted ending, are not contracted when they occur within the line.

Na konja nakladyvaet potniček	75,169
Na dobra konja podkladyvaet potniček	80,215

Only when the verb appears at the end of the line, as in lines 10-13 in No. 74, is the contracted form used.

Tak pexotoju nikto tut ne proxáživat,
Na dobrom koni nikto tut ne proézživat,
Ptica černoj voron ne prolétyvat,
Seryj zver' da ne prorýskivat.

The following verbs are typical of those which occur at the end of the line.

Uncontracted		Contracted	
lomáetsja	75,182	poígryvat	77,117
proxlažáetsja	75,539	pokídyvat	77,118
otvédaem	77,160	poézživaš'	79,14
znáete	79,101	potáptyvaš	79,15

xvástaet	79,210	slúšatsja	79,31
védaeš'	80,253	poxáživat	79,217
poxáživaet	81,65	vygovárivat	79,256
vygovárivaet	81,66	porozmáxivat	80,376
poézživaet	84,113	poxáživat	80,819
pod"ézživaet	84,116	pogovárivat	80,820
podxvátyvaet	84,117		

Slušatsja is the only form not containing the suffix yvaj which is contracted. If it were not contracted at the end of the line, the ending would contain three unstressed syllables. All the other forms which show contraction contain this suffix and are stressed on the penultimate syllable of the stem. If there were no contraction of the vowels in these verbs, the ending of the lines in which they occur would not have the dactylic ending which is characteristic of these bylina. Some lines end with verbs containing the -yvaj suffix but without contraction. They occur only in the bylina "Vol'ga i Mikula", "Dunaj", and "Xoten Bludovič", which contain metrical features which differentiate them from the other bylina. The uncontracted ending of -yvaj verbs is one of the chief ways of forming the ending with three unstressed syllables which is peculiar to these bylina. A verb in these bylina has the uncontracted form, while the contracted form of the same verb appears in the others.

poxáživaet	81,65	poxáživat	79,217
vygovárivaet	81,66	vygovárivat	79,256
poézživaet	84,113	poézživaš'	79,14
pod"ézživaet	84,116	pod"ézživat	77,115
podxvátyvaet	84,117	podxvátyvat	77,116

The fact that contraction occurs mainly in verbs having the -yvaj suffix, that such verbs appear only at the end of the line, and that uncontracted verbs in -yvaj appear at line end in bylina with special metrical characteristics shows that use of contracted or uncontracted verb endings is determined by metrical requirements.

5. REFLEXIVE SUFFIX

In the bylina of Rjabinin metrical requirements determine the form of the reflexive suffix in verb forms whose final sound, consonant or vowel, determines the shape of the suffix in contemporary literary usage. Both alternants of the suffix, -s' and -sja (-si) may occur with past tense verbs. Infinitives have only the full form, while participles occur only with the contracted form. The determining factor in the appearance of the full or the shortened form is not a final vowel or consonant but the place of the stress. The following verbs which occur at the end of the line demonstrate that the position of the stress conditions the usage.

Verbal Forms with -s'		Verbal Forms with -sja (-si)	

Past Tense, Feminine

75,616	pokónčilas'	77,17	nasmejálasja
77,308	porozdúmalas'	77,213	ostojálasi
80,796	ládilas'	79,168	molílasi
85,528	pozdoróvkalas'		

Past Tense, Neuter

		75,396	sljubílosi

Past Tense, Plural

75,251	pozdoróvkalis'	75,252	celoválisja
77,300	poroz"éxalis'	76,122	pomirílisja
80,380	klánjalis'	80,21	prituljálisja
80,528	rosslúxalis'	80,132	pomolílisja
85,61	stólnulis'	80,333	opletálisja
80,763	roz"éxalis'	80,334	osypálisja
80,849	porozslúxalis'	80,335	priklonjálisja
85,62	porostólnylis'	80,355	opustílisja
		80,794	učílisja
		85,351	priložílisja

Infinitives

		77,222	nasmexátisja
		77,304	proklaždátisja
		78,79	povinovátisja

Participles

80,311	sjádučis'
80,312	poédučis'
80,622	pivájučis'
81,208	priédučis'
81,425	pytájučis'

If the verbal form is stressed on the penultimate syllable, the full form of the suffix is used. If it is stressed on the antepenultimate syllable, the shortened form appears.

6. PLEOPHONY

Pleophonic and nonpleophonic forms of the same word appear in the *bylina*. Meter determines the use of one or the other of a pair of such words.

Za ego *za pérstni za zlačényi*	75,132
A j obručiki *nabíty zoločényi*	85,155
U nix krovel'ki vse *býli zoločényi*	85,470

In the first example the pleophonic form could have been used and there would have been three unstressed syllables between the main stresses. Although it is not strictly observed, the rule for repetition of prepositions calls for the repetition of *za*, since the adjective follows the noun. If *za* is repeated, the pleophonic form cannot be used, for four syllables would then separate the two stresses. By use of the nonpleophonic form the rule for repetition of prepositions can be followed, and the proper sequence of unstressed syllables is maintained. Since the last two examples are not parts of a prepositional phrase, there is no preposition to be repeated. A particle could be used with the nonpleophonic form, but the alternative of using the pleophonic form was chosen.

In the following examples the short adjective in the nonpleophonic form is stressed on the final syllable, the pleophonic adjective on the first. The examples show that the number of syllables in the noun determines which form of the adjective appears, since the third syllable from the end must be stressed.

On spustil tuda on svoj *zlačén persten'*	80,965
Da j skočila-to Nastas'ja čerez *žolot stol*	80,990

In the first of the following lines the stressed word preceding the pleophonic form is of one syllable; no unstressed syllable follows the stress. In the second example one unstressed syllable follows the stressed syllable in the word preceding the nonpleophonic form.

A j odežicu ty *brát' dorogocénnuju*	83,10
I odež'-ko ty moju *odéžu drogocénnuju*	75,476

A particle and a nonpleophonic form may be used as the equivalent of the pleophonic form.

Šli ony po *grádu-to po Kíevu*	80,138
Ko tomu ko *górodu ko Kíevu*	75,578

These examples show that the appearance of a word in its pleophonic or nonpleophonic form is influenced by the meter.

7. SUFFIXATION

Suffixes may be added to nouns which denote the relative size of an object or the attitude of the speaker toward the object. These suffixes usually contain one syllable. In comparable lines the use of the suffixed or unsuffixed noun affects the structure of the line. In the following examples a suffixed form is equivalent to the unsuffixed form and a pronoun.

Stal on bit' tu *síluška velíkuju*	75,369
Budeš' bit'-to *sílu tu velíkuju*	75,384
Tak ne smel on k *poljanícišču pod"éxati*	77,48
Da ne smel on k *poljaníce toj pod"éxati*	77,33

The relationship between a suffixed form and an unsuffixed form to the number of syllables preceding the stressed syllable of the following word may be seen from the following lines. There is one such syllable in the line containing the suffixed form, two in the one with the unsuffixed form.

Stal *odéžicy ottúlja* Djuk ponašivat'	85,272
Polagala-to *odéži snova-ná-novo*	85,256

There may be a difference in the place of the stress between the suffixed and unsuffixed forms, for example *golová – golóvuška*, accusative *gólovu – golóvušku*. In the lines which follow, both forms at the end of the line are preceded by the same adjective, the long form with the suffixed noun, the short with the unsuffixed one.

A srubit'-to *bújnuju golóvušku*	75,594
Otorvala by mne *bújnu gólovu*	75,573

In the first line the last two stresses are separated by the usual three syllables, by one in the second, which is allowed by the meter but is more uncommon. If the short adjective were used in the first line or the long in the second, the stresses would be separated by two syllables, a sequence which is avoided in this *bylina*.

The repetition of a preposition and the unsuffixed form alternate with the suffixed form without the repetition of the preposition in the following lines.

Vo tuju vo *sílušku velíkuju*	75,405
Molodoj sčenok da napustil na *sílu na velíkuju*	75,465
Da j po slavnu *po rozdól'icu čistú polju*	77,141
To on exal *po rozdól'ju po čistú polju*	77,129

8. WORD ORDER

The parts of the lines compared below are semantically identical, but the word order is different. The adjectives have the long or the short form depending on their position in the line.

Ty podí *v svoju stolóvuju vo górenku*	74,240
On skoren'ko šel *v stolóvu svoju górenku*	74,245
A j *bessčétnuju velíku* zolotu kaznu	83,9
Ix *velíkuju bessčétnu* zolotu kaznu	85,446

9 ALTERNATION OF PREPOSITIONS, PARTICLES, AND PRONOUNS

The following examples show the alternation of particles with each other, with pronouns, and with prepositions, all of which are used to attain the required distribution of stressed and unstressed syllables.

Podi-tko ty *k právomu ko strémeni* bulatnemu	80,508
Šol ko *právomu on strémeni* k bulatnemu	80,515
Da j na *slávnyj-ot počésten* pir	76,102
Da na moj-ot *slávnyj na počésten* pir	76,108
Posmotrel-to pod *vostóčnuju ved' stóronu*	75,212
Posmotrel-to pod *vostóčnuju on stóronu*	75,520
A j pod toj li pod *vostóčnoj pod storónuškoj*	75,521
A Vladymir *knjáz' da stol'ne-kíevskoj*	80,1
I tut Vladymir *knjáz'-ot stol'ne-kíevskoj*	80,38
Ty Vladymir *knjáz' naš stol'ne-kíevskoj*	80,99

VII

ACCENTUATION CHANGES AND THE FORMATION OF THE EPIC FORMULAS

1. INTRODUCTION

The usual ending of the *bylina* line is dactylic, and this rhythm is normally observed whatever the distribution of the stresses in the rest of the line. It is in the last half of the line where fixed phrases, the "epic formulas", such as *čistó pole* and *belú ruku* are most frequently found. In these combinations of adjective and noun, usually of two syllables each, the noun has lost its stress and has become enclitic to the preceding adjective. In expressions of the type *čistó pole*, moreover, the stress of the adjective is on the last syllable, while it is normally on the first. The adjective in *belú ruku* type phrases is regularly stressed on the last syllable so that the only change is the absence of stress on the noun.

2. ADJECTIVE-NOUN COMBINATIONS

Jakobson observes that the words which are enclitic in the epic formulas are those which had falling pitch in late Common Slavic. He states further that such formulas must have been fixed before the thirteenth century, since by that time rising and falling pitch were no longer distinguished in Russian.[1]

The epic formulas which follow are those which occur at the end of the line in the *bylina* of Rjabinin. Most formulas are found in this position, although they sometimes appear in other parts of the line, mainly at the beginning. Repetition of the last part of a line as the first part of the following line is a common stylistic device of the *bylina*. The formulas are presented according to the stem class of the noun and the accent type of the adjective (indefinite) and noun. Data for pitch in the paradigms are from Christian Stang, *Slavonic Accentuation*.[2]

[1] Roman Jakobson, "Studies in Comparative Slavic Metrics", *Oxford Slavonic Papers*, III (Oxford, 1952), p. 22
[2] Christian Stang, *Slavonic Accentuation* (Oslo, 1957).

2.1. *Root-Stressed Adjective and Mobile-Stressed Noun*

-ā Stems

sil'nja gora   Nominative singular. Short form feminine adjective now end-stressed. Noun stressed on final syllable. No retraction. Accentuation forms dactylic ending.

syru zemlju   Accusative singular. Stress retracted from falling tone.

syroj zemli   Genitive singular. Long form adjective end-stressed. Noun stressed on ending. No retraction. Accentuation forms dactylic ending.

levu nogu   Accusative singular. Stress retracted from falling tone.

pravu nogu   Accusative singular. Stress retracted from falling tone.

bystrym rekam   Dative plural. Long form adjective stressed on first syllable. Noun stressed on ending. No retraction. Accentuation by analogy to singular forms where retraction occurs, *Nepru reku*, etc.

levu ruku   Accusative singular. Stress retracted from falling tone.

pravu ruku   Accusative singular. Stress retracted from falling tone.

xorobru Litvu   Accusative singular. Stress probably retracted from falling tone.

xorobroj Litvy   Genitive singular. Long form adjective stressed on second syllable. Noun stressed on ending. No retraction. Accentuation by analogy to singular forms where retraction occurs.

-o, -jo Stems

syra duba   Genitive singular. Stress retracted from falling tone.

syru dubu   Dative singular. Stress retracted from falling tone.

syrom dubu   Prepositional singular. Long form adjective stressed on ending. Noun stressed on ending. Accentuation forms dactylic ending.

zlatu verxu   Dative singular. Stress retracted from falling tone.

zlatom verxu   Prepositional singular. Long form adjective and noun stressed on ending. Accentuation forms dactylic ending.

zlatom verxe   Prepositional singular. Stress retracted from falling tone.

zlaty verxi   Accusative plural. Stress retracted from falling tone.

zlatyx verxov   Genitive plural. Long form adjective and noun stressed on ending. No retraction. Accentuation forms dactylic ending.

-o, -jo Stems, Neuter

čisto pole   Accusative singular. Stress retracted from falling tone.

čista polja   Genitive singular. Stress retracted from falling tone.
čistu polju   Dative singular. Stress retracted from falling tone.
čistym polem   Instrumental singular. Stress retracted from falling tone.
čistym poljam   Dative plural. Long form adjective stressed on first syllable. Noun stressed on ending. No retraction. Accentuation by analogy to singular forms.

-i Stems

bož'ju cerkov'   Accusative singular. Long form adjective stressed on first syllable. Stress retracted from falling tone.
bož'ej cerkvi   Genitive singular. Long form adjective stressed on first syllable. Noun stressed on final syllable. No retraction. Accentuation by analogy to forms of singular where retraction occurs.
bož'ej cerkvi   Dative singular. Long form adjective stressed on first syllable. Stress retracted from falling tone.
bož'ej cerkvi   Prepositional singular. Long form adjective stressed on first syllable. Noun stressed on final syllable. No retraction. Accentuation by analogy to forms of singular where retraction occurs.
bož'i cerkvi   Nominative-accusative plural. Long form adjective stressed on first syllable. Stress retracted from falling tone.

2.2. *Mobile-Stressed Adjective and Mobile-Stressed Noun*

-o, -jo Stems, Masculine

čestnom piru   Prepositional singular. Long form adjective stressed on final syllable. Noun stressed on ending. No retraction. Accentuation forms dactylic ending.

-o, -jo Stems, Neuter

nagu telu   Dative singular. Stress retracted from falling tone.

2.3. *End-Stressed Adjective and Mobile-Stressed Noun*

-ā Stems

ključevu vodu   Accusative singular. Stress retracted from falling tone.
rezvy nogi   Accusative plural. Stress retracted from falling tone.
rezvy nožki   Accusative plural. Noun diminutive of *noga*, stressed on first syllable. No retraction. Accentuation by analogy to sin-

gular forms and nominative-accusative plural of *noga* where retraction occurs.

belu ruku   Accusative singular. Stress retracted from falling tone.

bely ruki   Accusative plural. Stress retracted from falling tone.

bely ručki   Accusative plural. Noun diminutive of *ruka*, stressed on first syllable. No retraction. Accentuation by analogy to singular forms and nominative-accusative plural of *ruka* where retraction occurs.

odnoj rukoj   Instrumental singular. Numeral stressed on final syllable. Noun stressed on ending. Accentuation forms dactylic ending.

odnoj ručkoj   Instrumental singular. Numeral stressed on final syllable. Noun diminutive of *ruka*, stressed on first syllable. No retraction. Accentuation by analogy to *odnoj rukoj* or forms of *ruka* where retraction occurs.

drugoj pory   Dative singular. Stress retracted from falling tone.

-o, -jo Stems, Masculine

krutoj bereg   Accusative singular. Stress retracted from falling tone.

vysok terem   Accusative singular. Stress retracted from falling tone.

odnym duxom   Instrumental singular. Stress retracted from falling tone.

edinym duxom   Instrumental singular. Stress retracted from falling tone.

belu svetu   Dative singular. Stress retracted from falling tone.

-o -jo Stems, Neuter

takovy slova   Accusative plural. Adjective and noun stressed on ending. Accentuation forms dactylic ending. In other *bylina* the singular *takovo slovo* is the most common form and shows stress retraction from the falling tone of the noun. The plural form has been substituted for the singular.

-i Stems

beloj grudi   Genitive singular. Noun stressed on last syllable. No retraction. Accentuation by analogy to forms where retraction occurs.

beloj grudi   Dative singular. Stress retracted from falling tone.

beloj grudi   Prepositional singular. Noun stressed on last syllable.

No retraction. Accentuation by analogy to forms where retraction occurs.

bely grudi   Accusative plural. Stress retracted from falling tone.

želty kudri   Accusative singular. Stress retracted from falling tone.

2.4. *Mobile-Stressed Adjective and End-Stressed Noun*

No retraction can have taken place in phrases with end-stressed nouns.

-ā Stems

čestna vdova   Nominative singular. Adjective and noun stressed on final syllable. Accentuation forms dactylic ending.

čestnoj vdovy   Genitive singular. Long form adjective stressed on final syllable. Accentuation forms dactylic ending.

zolota kazna   Nominative singular. Adjective stressed on final syllable. Accentuation forms dactylic ending.

zolotu kaznu   Accusative singular. Adjective stressed on first syllable. Accentuation by analogy to short forms stressed on endings or to long forms.

zolotoj kazny   Genitive singular. Adjective stressed on ending. Accentuation forms dactylic ending.

zolotoj kaznoj   Instrumental singular. Adjective and noun stressed on final syllable. Accentuation forms dactylic ending.

-o, -jo Stems, Masculine

zoloty vency   Accusative plural. Adjective stressed on first syllable. Noun stressed on final syllable. Accentuation by analogy to short forms stressed on ending or to long forms.

zoloty ključi   Accusative plural. Noun stressed on ending. Accentuation of adjective by analogy to short forms stressed on ending or to long forms.

-o, -jo Stems, Neuter

zelena vina   Genitive singular. Adjective stressed on first syllable. Accentuation could be due to dialect long forms stressed on end, analogous to *molodój – molódoj*.

2.5. *End-Stressed Adjective and End-Stressed Noun*

No retraction can have occurred in these combinations; the dactylic ending is formed without any change in the position of the stress.

-ā Stems

gorjuči slezy   Accusative plural.

-o, -jo Stems, Masculine

široka dvora   Genitive singular.

širokom dvore   Prepositional singular. Accentuation of adjective by analogy to short forms or the adjective may be a dialect form stressed on the ending.

tupom konce   Prepositional singular.

vostrym koncem   Instrumental singular. Accentuation probably by analogy to short forms.

dobra konja   Accusative genitive singular.

dobru konju   Dative singular.

dobrym konem   Instrumental singular. Long form adjective stressed on first syllable. Accentuation by analogy to short forms.

dobrom kone   Prepositional singular. Long form adjective stressed on first syllable. Accentuation by analogy to short forms.

dobryx konej   Genitive plural. Long form adjective stressed on first syllable. Accentuation by analogy to short forms.

dobryx konjax   Prepositional plural. Long form adjective stressed on first syllable. Accentuation by analogy to short forms.

bel šater   Accusative singular.

belu šatru   Dative singular.

bela šatra   Genitive singular.

belym šatram   Dative plural. Long form adjective stressed on first syllable. Accentuation by analogy to short forms.

melkim kuskam   Dative plural. Long form adjective stressed on first syllable. Accentuation unclear. Adjective may be stressed on ending in dialect.

krutym rebram   Dative plural.

velik zaklad   Accusative singular.

-o, -jo Stems, Neuter

bela lica   Genitive singular.

-i Stems

velika sažen'   Nominative singular.

No acute nouns show stress retraction in the epic formulas. The few phrases which contain nouns stressed on the first syllable and do not have the necessary conditions for stress retraction occur with adjectives stressed on the final syllable, *glubók pogreb, zlačén persten', veliká pjaden, svetél mesjac.*

2.6. *Enclitic Nouns*

Nouns which are enclitic may be end-stressed or mobile-stressed, while the adjectives to which the nouns are enclitic are root-, mobile-, or end-stressed. End-stressed nouns occur only with end-stressed adjectives or with the forms of mobile adjective paradigms which are stressed on the end. In these combinations there is no shift of stress, for both adjective and noun retain their original accentuation. In the rhythm of the line the adjective has a main stress, so the noun may be described as enclitic but only in a rhythmical sense. Mobile-stressed nouns are combined with all three adjective stress types. Since the mobile paradigm is the one which had circumflex intonation in the first syllable when other forms of the paradigm had the stress on the last,[3] on the evidence of the examples cited, retraction of stress to a preceding adjective occurred when the noun had falling intonation in the first syllable. Retraction takes place independently of the accentuation of the adjective. No examples of retraction of stress from an acute (root-stressed) noun are found.

3. ADJECTIVES WITH VARYING STRESSED SYLLABLES

The final syllable of the adjective in epic formulas must be stressed. Since this syllable is sometimes stressed when there can have been no retraction of stress from the noun and when the adjective is normally stressed on another syllable, at least in the literary language, the source of the accentuation can more probably be identified if the development of the stress patterns of adjectives is reviewed.

3.1. *Analogy in the Adjective Paradigm*

The indefinite adjectives were declined like nouns and the accent changes of the forms in the paradigm paralleled those of the nouns of the same declension. Accordingly there were root-stressed, end-stressed, and mobile-stressed adjectives. The definite forms of the root-stressed adjectives were also stressed on the root. End-stressed adjectives have

---

[3]   *Ibid.*, p. 21.

corresponding definite forms stressed on the syllable immediately preceding the ending. Stang assumes the following process:[4] *belàjego* becomes *belâgo*. The accent was on the last syllable of the stem, *a*, and with loss of *j* and contraction of the two vowels a long vowel with falling tone developed. Since the stress is retracted from a vowel with falling tone, *belâgo* becomes *bélago*. The case forms where no contraction took place, nominative-accusative singular, dual, and plural, acquired the same accentuation through analogy or by another kind of retraction. The long form of mobile-stressed adjectives may be stressed either on the stem or on the ending. When the first vowel of the stem had falling tone, the stress was advanced to the last syllable of the stem or to the enclitic which differentiates the long adjectives. If a long vowel with falling tone developed through contraction, the stress was retracted to the preceding syllable. Not all members of a paradigm would show retraction of the stress. The paradigm was then regularized, sometimes on the basis of forms which retracted the stress, sometimes on those which did not. Definite adjectives with mono-syllabic stems thus may be stressed on the stem syllable or on the first syllable of the ending. Adjectives with stems of more than one syllable may be stressed on the last stem syllable or on the first syllable of the ending.

It is possible for a mobile-stressed adjective to have a varying accentuation. It would be metrically advantageous for the narrator to have at his disposal the same form, but with the stress on different syllables. Such a situation may have existed, for some dialects still preserve adjectives with alternate stress patterns. Although most adjectives in *bylina* have the stress on the same syllable in all forms, there are some which have an alternating pattern. Thus *molodoj* may be stressed on any of the three syllables. The modern language has generalized the stress on the last syllable, but *molodój* and *molódoj* are used by Rjabinin. Since both forms are theoretically possible, it is probable that two "stress paradigms" existed in Rjabinin's *bylina* language, and perhaps in his dialect, as a result of generalizing on the basis of the forms with end stress, *molodój* and also of the forms with the stress on the preceding syllable, *molódoj*. Nahtigal cites the dialect form *molódyj*.[5] The form with the stressed first syllable, *mólodoj*, cannot be explained by a regular development of the language. Since the masculine and neuter, the plural, and some of the feminine short forms were stressed on the first syllable, it can be assumed that *mólodoj* is formed by analogy to these short forms.

[4] *Ibid.*, p. 101.
[5] R. Nahtigal, *Slavjanskie jazyki* (Moscow, 1963), p. 60.

3.2. *Definite and Indefinite Adjectives Stressed on the Same Syllable*

Some indefinite adjectives are stressed by analogy on the same syllable as the definite forms. The continued use of indefinite forms in attributive position in *bylina* after they had become restricted to the predicate in the spoken language could have contributed to the indefinite forms sometimes acquiring the stress of the definite forms. This could be the explanation of the stress in such phrases as *bélu grud'* from *béluju grud'*, *molodú ženu* from *molodúju ženu*, and *zolotý ključi* from *zolotýe ključi*.

4. ANALOGY IN FORMULA FORMATION

Most occurrences of the formulas containing the words *čistó pole* are in the singular where all cases of the noun have falling tone and retraction of stress to the final syllable of the adjective is regular. But the dative plural *čistým poljam* occurs where no retraction can have taken place since the noun was accented on the last syllable. The accentuation of the formula in the plural must be by analogy to the singular. The natural accentuation of combinations of end-stressed adjectives and nouns as in *dobrá konja* forms the dactylic ending. The long form *dóbryj* is stressed on the first syllable. The stress on the final syllable of the adjective in the instrumental and prepositional singular *dobrým konem* and *dobróm kone* is due to analogy with *dobrá konja*.

Models for analogy are phrases containing the same adjective and noun. The stress on the last syllable of the adjective *dobrým* in *dobrým konem* is by analogy to *dobrá konja* and not to the adjective *dobrá* alone. In this type of analogy there must be some forms of the adjective and noun combination whose natural accentuation forms the dactylic ending to serve as models. Models for analogy in formulas like *čistým poljam* are combinations of the same adjective and noun in which retraction occurred, as in *čistó pole*.

The original stress pattern of the epic formulas was formed by retraction of stress from nouns with falling tone on the first syllable. Analogy has occurred almost exclusively with those forms of the mobile paradigm which could not show retraction on the model of those which could. After this stress pattern was established, "new" epic formulas were formed from combinations of end-stressed nouns with end-stressed adjectives and with those forms of mobile adjectives stressed on the final syllable. No change in accentuation has occurred; there is only an ordering of stressed and unstressed syllables so that the third syllable from the end of the line (and the final syllable) is stressed.

5. EPIC FORMULAS FROM DIFFERENT LANGUAGE PERIODS

Korš has rightly pointed out that the language of folklore is a mixed one, containing as it does elements from different dialects and different stages in the development of the language.[6] Explanation of such aspects of the *bylina* as the epic formulas must take this fact into consideration. Some treatments of proclisis and enclisis in the formation of epic formulas are unsatisfactory because the kinds of proclisis and enclisis are not differentiated. Phrases of the type *čistó pole* and *belý ruki*, in which the stress of the noun is retracted to the adjective, are clearly old. Expressions such as *ruki bélye* also occur where the noun is said to be proclitic to the adjective. No change in the stress pattern has occurred, and in this respect they are similar to *dobrá konja* type phrases. All three types, *belý ruki*, *ruki bélye*, and *dobrá konja*, were possible at the time when *belý ruki* was formed. But only *ruki bélye* is a still living construction type in the modern language. After the restriction of short adjectives to the predicate, phrases like *dobrá konja* were possible only in the language of folklore, while *belý ruki* phrases have not been possible since Russian lost tonal distinctions. The noun in *belý ruki* is enclitic in the real sense because the stress was retracted from a falling tone to a preceding syllable. In *dobrá konja* and *ruki bélye* there is no real enclisis or proclisis since no change in accentuation has taken place. There is only a rhythmical subordination of one stress to another, and in the *bylina* the third syllable from the end of the line has a main stress. Therefore, stresses before or after this syllable are rhythmically subordinate to it. The three phrases may be called instances of enclisis or proclisis, but the formation of each has a different linguistic basis.

[6]   F. E. Korš, "O russkom narodnom stixosloženii", *Sbornik Otdelenija russkogo jazyka i slovesnosti*, LXVII, No. 8 (St. Petersburg, 1901), p. 46.

VIII

DEVELOPMENT OF THE LINE IN RUSSIAN

1. INTRODUCTION

A hypothetical early Slavic verse line can be constructed from the common features preserved in the verse of the several Slavic languages. It should be possible to trace the development of the Russian line by comparing it with this hypothetical one. The Proto-Slavic epic line as reconstructed by Jakobson has the following characteristics:[1]

1. A constant number of syllables (10).
2. Indifferent quantity of the final (tenth) syllable, which is preceded by a quantitative close: a long in the penult (ninth syllable) and shorts in the two preceding syllables (seventh and eight).
3. Lack of any regular pattern of quantity in the initial (first to sixth) syllables of the line.
4. A compulsory break (before the fifth syllable).

Comparison of the Russian and Serbo-Croatian lines should also help to explain the changes in the Russian line, since the epic tradition has been well preserved in Serbo-Croatian also.

In reviewing the changes which have affected the form of the Russian line, each change is treated separately so that a sequence of stages in the development of the line is obtained. These stages are not necessarily representations of lines which actually occurred. Some of them probably are, but it is unnecessary to assume that whole *bylina* were composed of them. Some of the changes probably occurred simultaneously or at least overlapped, so that some of the intermediate stages in the representation may never have existed, although they help to clarify the process of development. Moreover, the changes must have been gradual so that different forms of lines existed at the same time. Since the rhythm

---

[1] Roman Jakobson, "Studies in Comparative Slavic Metrics", *Oxford Slavonic Papers*, III (Oxford, 1952), p. 62.

in the earliest *bylina* which are available for study is already regular for each line type, the possible variant lines have been lost and a regular meter generalized to all lines. But evidence for the existence of earlier lines or parts of lines is preserved in the present stage of the development of the Russian epic line.

2. STRUCTURE OF THE EPIC LINE IN RUSSIAN AND SERBO-CROATIAN

According to Jakobson the rhythmic basis of the line in Proto-Slavic was vowel quantity. The only constant was a long vowel in the ninth syllable and short vowels in the seventh and eighth. Since Serbo-Croatian preserves differences in vowel quantity and intonations and has a free stress, the Serbo-Croatian line should more closely resemble the Proto-Slavic than the Russian, since Russian has preserved only free stress.

2.1. *Long Vowels in the Serbo-Croatian Line*

Jakobson's data from his study of the meter of the epic songs of T. Vučić may be used to exemplify the Serbo-Croatian meter. The percentage of long vowels in each syllable is given below:[2]

Syllable	1	2	3	4	5	6	7	8	9	10
Percentage	23	15	29	19	19	14	10	9	57	19

The high percentage of longs in the ninth syllable and the low percentage in the seventh and eighth agree with the distribution in the hypothetical Proto-Slavic line. There is a slight tendency for other odd syllables to be stressed also so that a faint trochaic rhythm emerges. In the final colon, the fifth to tenth syllables, the fifth and ninth syllables are the ones most likely to contain longs. In the line as a whole the third and the ninth syllables have the highest percentage. Since they are the penultimate syllables in each colon, the end of both colons is marked by a trochaic rhythm. The trochaic tendency is more pronounced in the first colon with the second and fourth syllables containing significantly fewer long vowels than the first and third.

2.2. *Stresses in the Serbo-Croatian Line*

Since Russian has retained only free stress, the distribution of the stresses in the Serbo-Croatian epic line could be more comparable to their distribution in the Russian line than is the distribution of long vowels.

[2]   *Ibid.*, p. 26.

Jakobson gives the following distribution of the stresses in Vučić's epic poetry:[3]

Syllable	1	2	3	4	5	6	7	8	9	10
Percentage	62	31	53	—	75	22	34	35	42	—

As with length, the stresses in the first colon tend also toward a trochaic distribution. The trochaic tendency is even more pronounced with stress than with the long vowels. The fifth and ninth syllables, which contain the largest percentage of longs in the final colon, are also the most frequently stressed. However, the percentage of stresses on the fifth syllable is greater than on the ninth, while the ninth has the greater number of long vowels. Unlike the distribution of long vowels, the percentage of stresses on the seventh and eighth syllables does not greatly differ from the percentage on the ninth. However, the percentage on the ninth is larger, which shows a tendency for the stressed ninth syllable to mark the end of the line.

The distribution of stresses in the first colon is more distinctly trochaic than in the second. There is also a stronger trochaic tendency in the distribution of the stresses than of the long vowels. The first syllable has the highest percentage of stresses in the first colon, whereas the third has the highest percentage of long vowels.

The distribution of both stress and vowel length tends to be trochaic, but stress has a stronger tendency to mark the beginning of the colons while length more definitely marks the end, at least of the final colon and therefore the line end. The complete absence of stress on the fourth and tenth syllables points up the stressed third and ninth syllables, so these sequences also mark the end of the colons.

2.3. *Similarity of Lines in Russian and Serbo-Croatian*

There are similarities between the distribution of the stresses in the Serbo-Croatian line and in the Russian eleven-syllable line, especially in the beginning of the line. In Serbo-Croatian the percentage of stresses on the first syllable is high, whereas it is usually unstressed in Russian. Jakobson connects this change with the development of a free dynamic stress in Russian.[4] Stress on the third syllable is a constant in the Russian line, and it is one of the most frequently stressed syllables in the Serbo-Croatian. The fourth syllable is unstressed in both. Stress on the fifth syllable in 75 percent of the Serbo-Croatian lines is the same

---

[3] *Ibid.*, p. 26.
[4] *Ibid.*, p. 40.

as the percentage of the eleven-syllable lines of Rjabinin. The break between the fourth and fifth syllables in Serbo-Croatian has been lost in Russian. From midline the Serbo-Croatian and Russian lines diverge in the use of stress. The sixth and eighth syllables are usually unstressed in Russian, unlike the Serbo-Croatian lines. The seventh syllable is more frequently stressed in Serbo-Croatian than in Russian. Stress on the ninth syllable is a constant in Russian but is stressed in fewer than half the Serbo-Croatian lines. Stress is the only prosodic feature in Russian which can be used as a basis of meter, and its distribution is regular throughout the line. Both stress and vowel length may be utilized in Serbo-Croatian; neither of them has a consistent distribution. The distribution of these two prosodic features was probably similar in the Old Russian lines, with stress assuming the basic role on the loss of vowel length.

2.4. *Comparison of Serbo-Croatian and Russian with Proto-Slavic*

The structure of both the Russian and Serbo-Croatian line differs from the hypothetical Proto-Slavic one, but the changes in Russian are much greater than in Serbo-Croatian. The Serbo-Croatian line, like the Proto-Slavic one, contains ten syllables, while lines of eleven and thirteen syllables are the most frequent in Russian. The distribution of long vowels in the close of the Serbo-Croatian line is similar to that in the Proto-Slavic line. The same tendency is observed in the distribution of stresses, with an unstressed final syllable and a higher frequency of stressed vowels in the ninth syllable than in the seventh and eighth. The Russian close differs markedly from the Proto-Slavic and the Serbo-Croatian. The final syllable is optionally stressed, the penultimate unstressed, and the third syllable from the end always stressed. The frequency of stress on the two syllables preceding the stress of the close is low as is the frequency of long vowels in Proto-Slavic and Serbo-Croatian. As in the Proto-Slavic line, the differences in frequency of long vowels in the first six syllables of Serbo-Croatian are too slight to create a clear metrical pattern, although odd syllables have higher frequencies. However, the stress frequencies for these syllables indicate a distinct trochaic rhythm. The Serbo-Croatian line differs in this respect from the Proto-Slavic line. The Russian line also differs from the Proto-Slavic and the odd syllables are stressed even more consistently than in the Serbo-Croatian. The Serbo-Croatian line has retained a break before the fifth syllable, while Russian has lost it.

Not only has the Russian line been lengthened, but a dactylic close has replaced the trochaic one of Proto-Slavic. Since the Serbo-Croatian line is trochaic and the Russian line is "trochaic" in the sense that odd syllables are stressed, this rhythmic tendency must have been inherited from Proto-Slavic. The discussion which follows attempts to show the development of the Russian epic line from a ten-syllable line with a trochaic rhythm, or at least a trochaic tendency, and with a break after the fourth syllable.

3. THE EPIC FORMULAS

3.1. *Original Position of Accent*

Before the shift of stress from the initial syllable of nouns with falling tone in the epic formulas, some of these phrases of adjective and noun had a trochaic ending. The adjective and the noun are almost always composed of two syllables each. The adjective usually has the short ending. The epic formulas often occur as prepositional phrases so that the total number of syllables in them is five.

vo čisto pole	–/–/–
na syru zemlju	–/–/–
na pravu nogu	–/–/–
vo bož'ju cerkov'	–/–/–

In other formulas the adjective was end-stressed.

na rezvy nogi	– –//–
vo belu ruku	– –//–
po belu svetu	– –//–

Both groups are similar in having a trochaic ending. In a third group of formulas both adjective and noun were end-stressed.

na dobra konja	– –/–/
ko belu šatru	– –/–/
so bela lica	– –/–/

The first two groups are roughly three times more numerous than the last.

Before the shift of stress to the last syllable of the adjective the rhythm of the last four syllables of the phrases in the first group was trochaic. The phrases of the second group agree in having a trochaic ending. Before a regular distribution of stresses throughout the line, these phrases may also have been in final position in the line. It is highly improbable that the third group could have been at the end of the line at an early time since accent on the ninth syllable was constant.

3.2. *Retraction of Stress*

The epic formulas occur most frequently at the end of the line. If they retain their original syntactical position, and the syntactic structure of Slavic languages is particularly conservative,[5] retraction of stress in phrases like those in the first two groups relocated the stress on the third syllable from the end of the line instead of the second. The ending became dactylic instead of trochaic in lines of this type. Furthermore, the syllable to which the stress was retracted was probably lengthened so that not only the place of stress but the long vowel as well conflicted with the trochaic tendency of the line.

Considering the overall tendency toward a trochaic line, it might be concluded that the conflict of the rhythm of the epic formulas with the rhythmic tendencies of the line would lead to their elimination or else their appearance in another part of the line where they would agree with the meter. Since they contain five syllables they could occur only in the last colon, if the colons were of four and six syllables and if the break in the line had not been lost or relocated before this time. It is more probable that the loss of the break was a later development. There is no compelling reason to assume that the epic formulas originally occurred in another part of the line. Because of their rhythm and the number of syllables they contain, it may be concluded that they retained their original position after retraction of stress and that the resulting dactylic ending was generalized in all lines.

3.3. *Epic Formulas Without Stress Retraction*

The question of the *dobrá konja* phrases remains. The stress in these phrases has not been retracted. Since their rhythm does not fit the original trochaic rhythm of the line end, their occurrence in this position must be secondary. Only after the dactylic ending was established could phrases of this type appear at the end of the line. The final syllable of these phrases is stressed, but this stress does not conflict with the dactylic ending, for stress on the final syllable of the ending is optional.

[5]   Roman Jakobson, "The Kernel of Comparative Slavic Literature", *Harvard Slavic Studies* (Cambridge, 1953), p. 29.

3.4. Rhythmic Similarity of Epic Formulas and Adjectives with Uncontracted Endings

Jakobson states that uncontracted forms of the definite adjectives were preserved at the end of the line because they meet the demands of the meter for a dactylic ending.[6] These endings are preserved inside the line as well, and their form varies according to the syllabic and rhythmical structure of the adjoining words. Before the development of the dactylic ending, adjectives could occur at the end of the line if they had monosyllable endings and would form a trochaic close. Only after the dactylic ending had been formed by retraction of stress in the epic formulas could the same adjectives with disyllabic endings appear at the end of the line. Once they had appeared in this position, the retention of the disyllabic ending would have been supported by the rhythm of the line end. For example, the expression *vo belý ruki* occurs frequently at the end of the line. It shows loss of stress of the noun and must be an old formation. But *vo belý ruki* occasionally alternates with *v ruki bélye* which contains no feature to indicate that it is an old construction. No change in accentuation has taken place. A direct order *bélye rúki* cannot appear at the end of the line, for the ending would then be trochaic. But by reversing the order the disyllabic ending of the adjective forms the necessary dactylic close. Thus it is more likely that adjectives with disyllabic endings, those with uncontracted endings also, appeared in final position because of the identity of the rhythm of the endings with the rhythm of the epic formulas after stress retraction.

4. EFFECT OF FORMATION OF FORMULAS ON LINE STRUCTURE

The Russian epic line has lost the fixed break after the fourth syllable. In Jakobson's view the break was eliminated as a result of the conflict of dichotomy and trichotomy in the line.[7] The line was divided into two parts but contained three sense groups, one in the first colon, two in the second. Each sense group contained one stress.

4.1. Tendency toward Sequences of Three Unaccented Syllables

In Vučić's epic lines the sixth, seventh, and eighth syllables contain the smallest percentage of long vowels. The sixth syllable also contains

[6]   Roman Jakobson, "O sootnošenii meždu pesennoj i razgovornoj narodnoj reč'ju", *Voprosy jazykoznanija*, No. 3 (Moscow, 1962), p. 89.
[7]   Jakobson, "Studies", *op. cit.*, p. 48.

the smallest percentage of stressed vowels. Only the second syllable has a smaller percentage of stressed vowels than the seventh and eighth. Although the percentage in the seventh syllable should be greater than in the eighth since the rhythm is trochaic, the percentage in the eighth is actually higher. As a result the trochaic rhythm is manifested in the second colon by the fifth and ninth syllables. In terms of both stress and length the sixth, seventh, and eighth syllables are rhythmically weak since their contribution toward maintaining a trochaic rhythm is negligible. There are three syllables between the fifth and ninth. Since this interval of weak syllables between strong syllables is the one most often observed in Russian epic lines, this tendency must have existed in the Proto-Slavic line in the final colon and must have been preserved after the formation of the dactylic ending in the Russian line.

The strong syllable at the end of the line after the change to a dactylic ending was the eighth and not the ninth, as in the Serbo-Croatian and Proto-Slavic lines. To maintain the three-syllable interval between strong syllables, stressed in Russian, the fourth syllable would have to become a strong one instead of the fifth. But this syllable is part of the first colon. Furthermore, the third syllable must be a strong one, and two strong syllables cannot be adjoining ones. The changes may be represented schematically. "s" designates strong syllables (stressed in Russian, stressed and/or long in Serbo-Croatian), "w" weak ones. "S" and "W" indicate conflicting tendencies in positions of strong and weak syllables.

Syllable	1	2	3	4	5	6	7	8	9	10
Serbo-Croatian	s	w	s	w	s	w	w	w	s	w
Russian with dactylic ending	s	w	s	w	s	W	W	s	w	w
New 3-syllable weak sequence	s	w	S	S	w	w	w	s	w	w
Subordination of one strong syllable	s	w	s	W	W	W	W	s	w	w

The rhythmic tendency of the first part of the line is to stress the third syllable, but the tendency of the last part is to stress the fourth. The tendencies of the two parts of the line conflict. If the tendency of the first part predominates, two weak syllables separate the last two strong ones and violate the trochaic rhythm. If the tendency of the end of the line is stronger and the fifth syllable becomes a weak one, the fourth must also be weak because it would be subordinated by the third which is always strong. Four weak syllables would then separate the only two strong syllables in the line, the third and eighth. This interval also interrupts the trochaic rhythm. A trochaic rhythm is impossible in such a line. Since the third, fifth, and ninth syllables in the most similar Russian line, of eleven syllables, are strong and the line still has a dactylic ending, the rhythmic tendencies of the Proto-Slavic and Serbo-Croatian line must have been preserved in Russian by adding an additional syllable to the line so that a trochaic rhythm is possible.

4.2. *Relocation of the Break*

This was the solution ultimately adopted, but one which may have been possible before the development of strong stress in Russian is the moving of the break so that it follows the fifth syllable. The syllabic structure of the epic formulas and the frequency of a five syllable colon suggest that such a line may have been an intermediate stage between the ten-syllable Proto-Slavic line with a break after the fourth syllable and the eleven-syllable Russian line without a fixed break.

By placing the break after the fifth syllable, a trochaic rhythm is possible in each colon, though not in the line as a whole. As Russian developed a strong dynamic stress the third syllable became the first strong one and not the first as in Serbo-Croatian. The two strongest syllables, constants, would then be the third and the eighth. After the break was moved, the tendency to avoid beginning a colon with a stressed syllable would further decrease the frequency of stress on the sixth syllable. The proximity of both the fifth and sixth syllables to strong syllables, the third and eighth, would contribute to their tendency to be unstressed or to contain words with secondary stress (pronouns, adverbs). This line would resemble those ten and eleven syllable lines in *bylina* which have two main stresses and are thus divided into two parts, 5-5 (--/-- --/--) and 5-6 (--/-- ---/--). Sreznevskij considers a ten-syllable line with two stresses, one in each of the two five-syllable parts, to be one of the oldest epic lines of all the Slavs. As an example he gives *už kak pal tuman na sine more*.[8] The structure of this line is the same as the hypothetical intermediate line between the 4-6 line and a Russian line without a break.

4.3. *Loss of the Break*

However, a line of two five-syllable parts is not trochaic. If the line should contain three stresses, two of them would have to be separated

---

[8] I. I. Sreznevskij, *Mysli ob istorii russkogo jazyka* (Moscow, 1959), p. 71.

by two syllables. *Bylina* lines with even numbers of syllables cannot be trochaic, but as a rule there is never more than one sequence with an even number of syllables, which shows that the trochaic tendency exists in lines with even numbers of syllables also. "Trochaic" is used here to mean only that stress occurs so that there are odd numbers of syllables in the most possible unstressed sequences. This persistent rhythmic tendency must have caused restructuring so that a trochaic rhythm could be realized throughout the line. One result was the loss of the fixed break.

4.4. *Expansion of the Line*

The trochaic line could have been restored by eliminating the dactylic close, but this solution was not carried out. Another alternative is to increase the number of syllables in the line. The Russian eleven-syllable epic line shows that this was the resolution of the rhythmic conflict. It is Jakobson's opinion that the first increase in the number of syllables was at the end of the line.[9] This cannot be the case if the dactylic ending was formed before the expansion of the line. If the dactylic ending were formed in a ten-syllable line and the ending were preserved, expansion must begin within the line.

The connective particle *da* almost always precedes a five syllable phrase at the end of a line, very often an epic formula. Fourteen percent of the total number of lines have *da* in this position, while the percentage in other positions is only 2 percent. The restriction of *da* to this position, connecting two five-syllable colons, cannot be by chance and must reflect an older form of the line without the particle. The presence of *da* in this position supports the hypothesis of the existence of a line with two five-syllable colons as well as indicating that the extra syllable was added between the two colons, thus replacing the break and forming an eleven syllable line. The following lines illustrate the appearance of the particle in this position.

Govorit Il'ja *da* takovy slova	75,242
I on vystal li *da* na rezvy nogi	75,250
A j na slavnoej *da* na Pučaj reki	79,90
Podat' knjazju-to *da* vo bely ruki	79,318
On na matušku *da* na syru zemlju	79,390

The first expansion of the ten-syllable line could have been by means

[9] Jakobson, "Studies", *op. cit.*, p. 48.

of this particle. The meaning of the line would not have been changed, but the line would have the necessary number of syllables to be trochaic. These lines would then be the models for the formation of an eleven-syllable line with a trochaic rhythm or at least with all the stresses on odd-numbered syllables. The substitution of *da* by other monosyllabic particles, pronouns, and similar words could have been the second stage in the formation of a regular eleven-syllable line.

A Vladymir knjaz' *da* stol'ne-kievskoj	80,1
I tut Vladymir knjaz'-*ot* stol'ne-kievskoj	80,38
Ty Vladymir knjaz' *naš* stol'ne-kievskoj	85,99
A Vladymir knjaz' *ty* stol'ne-kievskoj	80,957

The most frequent line in Rjabinin's *bylina* contains thirteen syllables. Jakobson states that the twelve- and thirteen-syllable lines were derived from the eleven by the addition of syllables between the third and fifth syllables.[10]

11	Kak vo stol'nom gorode vo Kieve
12	Kak vo stol'nom *vo* gorode vo Kieve
13	Kak vo stol'nom *bylo* gorode vo Kieve

Twelve-syllable lines are rare in the *bylina* of Rjabinin, and the thirteen-syllable may not have been expanded from a twelve-syllable line but directly from an eleven-syllable one. The following thirteen-syllable lines in the *bylina* of Rjabinin are derived from eleven-syllable ones.

Nad moim dvorom da nad vdovinyim	80,759
I nad moim-*to ved'* dvorom da nad vdovinyim	80,729
Govorit on s knjazem, ne mešaetsja	80,75
I govorit-*to* on *so* knjazem, ne mešaetsja	80,51
Govoril Il'ja da takovy slova	74,221
Govoril-*to on* Il'ja da takovy slova	74,71
U moej-to rodnoju u matuški	85,153
U moej *li* to *u* rodnoju u matuški	85,181

The thirteen-syllable lines are obtained by adding particles, prepositions, and pronouns between the third and fifth syllables of the eleven-syllable lines. Prepositions may occur in any position, except those where main stresses occur. Pronouns may also occasionally occur in strong position.

---

[10] *Ibid.*, p. 42.

The particle *to* occurs more frequently than any other. It also may occur in any syllable which does not have a main stress, but in the thirteen-syllable lines of "Dobrynja i Zmej", "Djuk", and "Dobrynja i Vasilij Kazimirov" over 80 percent of the occurrences are in the fourth, fifth, and sixth syllables. It is most frequent in the fourth syllable, less so in the fifth, and still less in the sixth. In eleven-syllable lines it occurs more frequently in the fourth syllable, but only half the total occurrences are in this syllable. In "Dobrynja i Zmej" and "Djuk" *to* occurs twice as frequently in the thirteen-syllable lines as in the eleven, while in "Dobrynja i Vasilij Kazimirov" the occurrence is almost three times as great as in the eleven-syllable line. *to* occurs in the expected positions for an eleven-syllable line to be expanded to a thirteen-syllable one and occurs more frequently in the thirteen-syllable lines than in the eleven-syllable lines. In addition to *to* the particles *tko, ka, li, ved'* may occur in these positions also. The predominance of thirteen-syllable lines and the expansion of eleven-syllable lines to thirteen-syllables is a result of the tendency to have three unstressed syllables between main stresses instead of one as in a strictly trochaic line.

APPENDIX

EXAMPLES OF LINES

GROUP 1

7	--/ -/--	Stal Vol'gá pokrýkivati		73,158
11Ia	--/ -/- --/--	Govoríl Mixájly takový slova		79,242
11Ib	--/- /- --/--	Prinosíla plát'e skomoróvčato		80,788
11Ic	--/ -/-- -/--	Molodój Dobrýnjuška Mikítinič		78,10
11Id	--/- /-- -/--	Da j červónym zólotom obvívano		80,222
11II	--/-- ---/--	So Opráksiej da korolévičnoj		76,112
11IIIa	--/- -/ --/--	Za stolóm-to sidját zatuljálisja		81,24
11IIIb	--/ --/ --/--	Aj že tý molodój skomoróšina		80,914
11IIIc	--/- -/- -/--	Da j na rús'skix mogúčix bogátyrej		81,4
11IIId	--/-- /- -/--	Da u rátoja sóška klenóvaja		73,47
11IIIe	--/ --/- -/--	A živút mužikí tam rozbójniki		73,70
11IIIf	--/- -/-- /--	A sxvatíl en tatárina zá nogi		81,193
15Ia	--/- /-- -/- --/--	Net živá-to stárogo kazáka Il'i Múromca		75,109
15Ib	--/ -/-- -/- --/--	Čto že tý xolópina dvorjánska porosxvástalsja		85,193
15Ic	--/- /- --/- --/--	En skorén'ko šól da po stolóvoj svoej górenki		80,39
15Id	--/ -/-- --/- --/--	K molodój knjagíne ko Nastas'e ko Mikúličnoj		80,777
15Ie	--/- /-- -/-- -/--	Im poéxat' nádobno k obédenke xristóvskoju		85,280
15If	--/ -/-- -/-- -/--	Ja stojál zaútrenu xristóvskuju vo Múromli		74,168
15Ig	--/ -/- --/-- -/--	Položíl zalógom svoju bújnuju golóvušku		80,431
15IIa	--/-- -/- /- --/--	Emu výbito ved' právo óko so kosíčeju		74,201

15IIb —/— —/— /— —/— Esli búde priletát'-to gólub so
golúbuškoj   80,289

15IIc —/— —/ —/— —/— Médnoe gvozd'é u nás tak
ne uščípletsja   85,126

15IId —/— —/ —/— —/— Móg by poberéč' Opráksu
korolévičnu   75,16

15IIe —/— —/— /— —/— I čto veleno očístit' úlicy streléckii 75,70

15IIf —/— —/— /— —/— Da j nastávit' po vsemú-to
ǵorodu po Kíevu   75,87

15IIg —/— —/ —/— —/— Ńekomu stoját' za cérkvi ved'
za bóžii   75,111

15IIh —/— —/ —/— —/— Prikazál on nakryvát' na stó-
liki dubóvyi   85,551

15IIIa —/— —/— —/— Priletéli-to podáročki da nel-
jubímyi   75,563

15IIIb —/— —/— —/— Prinestí-to velel plát'ico da sko-
moróvčato   80,745

15IV   —/— —/— —/— Ty posmátrivaj-tko na saxárne moe
dérevce   80,288

19Ia   —/— —/— —/ —/— —/— Tut pošlí-to dobry mó-
lodcy v svoí poláty belokámenny   80,149

19Ib   —/— —/— —/— /— —/— Prjamoézžeju doróžen-
koj ja éxal mímo-to Černígov grad   74,172

19IIa —/— —/— —/— —/— Posyláet on dvenádcat'-
to bogátyrej da svjatorús'skiix   85,448

19IIb —/— —/— —/— —/— Na vse ná tri na četýre
na storónuški da nizko klánjalis'   80,380

19III —/— —/— —/— —/— Knjázju-to Vladýmiru
da so Opráksoj korolévičnoj   75,273

GROUP 2

8a   —/ —/— Aj že Vol'gá Svjatoslávgovič   73,65

8b   —/— —/— Aj že Ofím'ja kupéc'-doči   84,142

8c   —/— /— Aj že moí slugi vérnyi   81,187

12Ia —/— —/— —/— Na prekrásnoj Opráks'i korolévičnoj   81,72

12Ib —/— /— —/— Ponizéšen'ku knjázju poklon-
jáetsja   81,31

12Ic —/ —/— —/— Kak-to stál mužičíšče derevénščina 80,797

12Id --/- -/-- -/-- Molodágo Ivánuška Dubróviča 80,83

12Ie --/-- /-- -/-- A Vasíl'juška párobka zamórskogo 81,125

12If --/ --/-- -/-- Za togó za Dunájuška Ivánoviča 81,310

12IIa --/-- -/ --/-- Pripečálivši pošlá prikručínivši 84,40

12IIb --/- --/ --/-- Nasmejálas' nado mnój čestnajá
vdova 84,67

12IIc --/-- -/- -/-- U rátoja kobýlka solóven'ka 73,46

12IId --/- --/- -/-- On sadílsja na kobýlku solóven'ku 73,85

16a --/- -/-- -/- --/-- Ne búdy služít' tobe sobáke
carju Kálinu 75,487

16b --/-- /-- -/-- -/-- Síl'nii rússkii mogúčii bogátyrja 81,56

20a --/ --/- --/-- -/- --/-- Xotját obnevólit' oni
stárago kazáka Il'ju Múromca 75,497

20b --/- -/-- -/-- -/-- -/-- Da v kói gusélyški to
s mólodu Dobrýnjuška poígryval 80,720

GROUP 3

9Ia --/- --/-- Kak ot ržán'ja lošadínago 75,197

9Ib --/-- -/-- A j Vasíl'juško Kazímirov 80,559

9II --/ -/- /-- A stoít sobáka Kálin car' 75,268

13a --/-- -/- --/-- Ena éxala sobáka nasmejálasja 77,17

13b --/- --/- --/-- Po vsem slávnym pereúlkam knja-
ženéckiim 78,7

13c --/-- -/-- -/-- Ko Ivánušku Godínovu pogljá-
dyvat' 83,124

13d --/- --/-- -/-- To Nastás'ja korolévična molí-
lasja 81,405

17a --/-- -/-- -/- --/-- Porozgnévalsja na stárago
j Kazáka Il'hu Múromca 75,2

17b --/- --/-- -/- --/-- Prikaží-tko izobrát' mne-ka
mestéčko na čestnóm piru 80,823

17c --/-- -/- --/- --/-- Pošel síluški velíkoj u
tatár da pootvédati 80,569

17d --/- --/- --/- --/-- Na vse ná tri na četýre na
storónki poklonílisja 85,504

17e --/-- -/-- -/-- -/-- Da j vo slávnogo bogátyrja
v Olóšen'ku Popóviča 80,194

17f --/- --/-- -/-- -/-- Stanet gólub so golúbuškoj
na dérevce progúrkivat' 80,290

17g --/-- -/- --/-- -/-- Ešče ètoe by znála bezvre-
mén'išče velíkoe   80,187

17h --/- --/- --/-- -/-- Na vse ná tri na četýre na
storónuški on klánjalsja   85,78

21a --/- --/-- -/-- -/- --/-- A j koról'-ot polagáet
on velíkuju bessčétnu zolotú kaznu   80,429

21b --/-- -/-- -/-- -/-- -/-- Po pravú ruku Vladý-
mira stojál-to ved' molóden'koj Dobrýnjuška   85,83

21c --/- --/-- -/-- -/-- -/-- Ešče čtó že polagáeš'
ty trinádcatyj to pódprug da zapásnyi   80,233

21d --/-- -/-- -/- --/-- -/-- Posmotrét' xotit na
síl'niex na rússkix na mogúčiix bogátyrej   85,10

25   --/-- -/-- -/- --/-- -/- --/-- Ivánuško Godí-
novič on édet po pravú ruku Nastás'i Mitriévičnoj   83,75

GROUP 4

10I   --/-- --/-- Na Opráksii korolévičnoj   81,355

10IIa --/ -/- -/-- Molodój Vasílej Kazímirov   81,157

10IIb --/- /- -/-- Moegó-to brátca krestóvogo   81,124

10IIc --/ -/-- /-- Usmotrél Xotínuška Blúdovič   84,47

14Ia   --/-- --/- --/-- A Vasíl'juško to sadílsja v go-
lový licem   81,276

14Ib   --/-- --/-- -/-- A Opráksija korolévična poxá-
živaet   81,222

14II   --/-- -/-- --/-- Ponizéšen'ko Vladýmiry pok-
lonjáetsja   81,116

14IIIa --/- -/ -/- --/-- A búdu stoját' za cérkvi za
gospódnii   75,490

14IIIb --/- -/ -/-- -/-- A j dólžen tut být' xolópina
dvorjánskaja   85,104

18   --/ -/- -/-- -/-- -/-- Oní vozmút-to privjážut
kak Ivánušku Godínova   83,91

A SELECTED BIBLIOGRAPHY

Astaxova, A. M., *Byliny* (Moscow-Leningrad, 1966).

Bulaxovskij, L. A., *Istoričeskij kommentarij k russkomu jazyku* (Kiev, 1958).

Evgen'eva, A. P., *Očerki po jazyku russkoj ustnoj poèzii v zapisjax XVII-XX vv.* (Moscow, Leningrad, 1963).

Gil'ferding, A. F., *Onežskie byliny*, 3 vols. (Moscow, Leningrad, 1949).

Goloxvastov, P. D., *Zakony stixa, russkogo narodnogo i našego literaturnogo* (St. Petersburg, 1883).

Harkins, William, "O metričeskoj roli slovesnyx formul v serboxorvatskom i russkom èpose", *American Contributions to the Fifth International Congress of Slavists* (The Hague, 1963).

Jakobson, Roman, "The Kernel of Comparative Slavic Literature", *Harvard Slavic Studies*, I (Cambridge, 1953).

——, "O sootnošenii meždu pesennoj i razgovornoj narodnoj reč'ju", *Voprosy jazykoznanija*, No. 3 (Moscow, 1962).

——, "Studies in Comparative Slavic Metrics", *Oxford Slavonic Papers*, III (Oxford, 1952).

Korš, F. E., "O russkom narodnom stixosloženii", *Sbornik Otdelenija russkogo jazyka i slovesnosti*, LXVII, No. 8 (St. Petersburg, 1901).

Mansikka, V., "O govore Šenkurskogo uezda Arxangel'skoj gubernii", *Izvestija Otdelenija russkogo jazyka i slovesnosti*, XVII, Book 2 (St. Petersburg, 1912).

Maslov, A. L., "Byliny, ix proisxoždenie, ritmičeskij i melodičeskij sklad", *Trudy Muzykal'no-ètnografičeskoj komissii* (Moscow, 1911).

Nahtigal, R., *Slavjanskie jazyki* (Moscow, 1963).

Sreznevskij, I. I., *Mysli ob istorii russkogo jazyka* (Moscow, 1959).

Stang, Christian, *Slavonic Accentuation* (Oslo, 1957).

Štokmar, M. P., *Issledovanija v oblasti russkogo narodnogo stixosloženija* (Moscow, 1952).

Taranovski, Kiril, *Ruski dvodelni ritmovi* (Belgrade, 1953).

——, Review of M. P. Štokmar, *Issledovanija v oblasti russkogo narodnogo stixosloženija* (Moscow, 1952). *Južnoslovenski filolog*, 21 (1955-1956).

Unbegaun, B. O., *Russian Versification* (Oxford, 1956).

Vasil'ev, L., "Jazyk belomorskix bylin", *Izvestija Otdelenija russkogo jazyka i slovesnosti*, VII, Book 4 (St. Petersburg, 1902).

Vostokov, A., *Opyt o russkom stixosloženii* (St. Petersburg, 1817).

Žirmunskij, V. M., *Introduction to Metrics*, trans. C. F. Brown (The Hague, 1966).

——, "The Versification of Majakowski", *Poetics, Poetyka, Poètika*, II (Warsaw, 1966).

INDEX

SLAVISTIC PRINTINGS AND REPRINTINGS

Edited by C. H. van Schooneveld

MOUTON · PUBLISHERS · THE HAGUE